Pr

Dear Heroin: A Memoir of Goodbyes is the poignant story of a mom, Linda, and her journey with her beloved son, Mikey, who after four years of struggling with his addiction to heroin (eight treatment centers, a total of twenty-three months of sobriety—fourteen months and nine months), in his desperation ended his life.

Linda does an excellent job of detailing the experience of a parent riding on the roller coaster ride of her young son caught up in the throes of the evil of addiction. Through the pain of it all, she remembers the amazing life of Mikey and all the sphere of friends he made an impact on. For any parent struggling with an addicted child or who has lost a child through addiction, this book will help you know you are not alone in the struggle of your journey and grief. Knowing you are not alone is the most comforting thing of all.

—Dr. Trudy Johnson, LMFT, CCTS-I
founder, A'nesis Retreats and Counseling Sabbaticals

Linda Morrison compassionately and clearly articulates the rugged journey of loving a son whose struggle with addiction reshapes their family life. *Dear Heroin* is a beautifully written chronicle which delves into the wilderness of loving and supporting a beloved family member who is also an addict. Morrison, through the lens of a "normal" middle class family, captures the depths of heartache and the hope of periods of sobriety and recovery, in a way that moves deep inside of the story statistics tell. This is a mother's tale of the courage it takes to look at hard truths, both for herself and for her son. You will feel the special light of her son Mike, especially in his grace periods of sobriety. This rich and multi-layered story conveys how much he wanted to be a full human being and how many hearts he touched along the way. In the end, the fierce love of his family could not hold him in this world and he took his own life, via heroin.

This is a tale of survival, of the difficult, searing walk through grief into gratitude and hope. Linda Morrison and her family have emerged on the other side of this loss; marked by it, yes, but also here to share the miracle of feeling joy and laughter again, of finding abundance after unimaginable loss. In a world where opioid addiction is a growing crisis, *Dear Heroin* will illumine a healing path for others who are touched by this particular brand of loss and for those who wish to understand such a journey.

—Patricia Hoolihan, author of six books including her memoir, *Storm Prayers: Retrieving and Reimagining Matters of the Soul,* and recently released *Hands and Hearts Together: Daily Meditations for Caregivers*; instructor at the Loft Literary Center, Minneapolis, MN; writing instructor at Metropolitan State University, Saint Paul, MN

This powerful and inspirational book tells the story of a mother, and her family, who unsuspectingly step into the web-like world of heroin addiction. It is also a timeless love story of a mother for her son. Linda Morrison's fight to save her beloved son, Michael, from heroin never falters even during the many times that his recovery seems hopeless. Along with the support of family, friends, personal faith, and professional help, she discovers strengths within herself that help her through four excruciating years of emotional turmoil and heartbreak. This memoir is invaluable to anyone seeking to understand someone with an opioid addiction, how addiction progresses, and how it ultimately destroys trust, the bedrock of relationships. In addition, it demystifies the perplexing process of seeking treatment.

When Michael dies by suicide, one horrific journey ends and another begins: a journey of loss whose pain has no words and a path that does not end. Nevertheless, Linda Morrison does not abandon herself or us to despair. Rather her resilience rises again, revealing a message of transcendence: That hope comes from fighting with a vengeance for those we love, addicted or sober, living or deceased.

—Judith Sullivan, author of *The Terrifying Wind: Seeking Shelter Following the Death of a Child*

This is a powerful story of addiction, suicide, faith, and recovery told as a first-hand account of one who has made the painful trek. Linda's gripping account of her youngest son's life in addiction and their family's journey alongside him is very raw, relatable, and real. A must read for parents, loved ones, or those suffering in the painful throes of addiction or the aftermath of suicide.

—Richard Bahr, chaplain, homeless advocate, and author of *Those People: The True Character of the Homeless*

Dear Heroin

Dear Heroin
Dear Heroin
Dear Heroin
Dear Heroin
Dear Heroin
Dear Heroin

A Memoir of Goodbyes

Phil,
Thank you for your support & encouragement.
Linda

Linda Morrison

WISE INK

ISBN 13: 978-1-63489-420-3

Library of Congress Catalog Number has been applied for.
Printed in the United States of America
First Printing: 2021

25 24 23 22 21 5 4 3 2 1

Cover design by Emily Mahon
Interior design by Patrick Maloney

Wise Ink Creative Publishing
807 Broadway St NE
Suite 46
Minneapolis, MN, 55413

Some names and identifying details have been changed to protect the privacy of individuals.

This book is dedicated to:

My son Michael Thomas, a great warrior who lost his battle with addiction; the thousands of warriors who have lost their battles; and those who are still in the heat of this conflict.

All of the loving families who have fought valiantly beside their sons and daughters, their siblings, their spouses, parents, grandparents, or friends.

All families currently on the front lines of this devastating disease. I have been where you are. I know your pain, your sorrow, and your losses. I stand beside you, not knowing how or when the tide may turn in favor of you or your loved one.

I want you to know you are not alone.

Contents

Part Three

Ailey, Baldwin, Floyd, Killens, and Mayfield

When great trees fall,
rocks on distant hills shudder,
lions hunker down
in tall grasses,
and even elephants
lumber after safety.

When great trees fall
in forests,
small things recoil into silence,
their senses
eroded beyond fear.

When great souls die,
the air around us becomes
light, rare, sterile.
We breathe, briefly.
Our eyes, briefly,
see with
a hurtful clarity.
Our memory, suddenly sharpened,
examines,
gnaws on kind words
unsaid,
promised walks
never taken.

Great souls die and
our reality, bound to
them, takes leave of us.
Our souls,
dependent upon their
nurture,
now shrink, wizened.
Our minds, formed
and informed by their
radiance,
fall away.
We are not so much maddened
as reduced to the unutterable ignorance
of dark, cold
caves.

And when great souls die,
after a period peace blooms,
slowly and always
irregularly. Spaces fill
with a kind of
soothing electric vibration.
Our senses, restored, never
to be the same, whisper to us.
They existed. They existed.
We can be. Be and be
better. For they existed.

—Maya Angelou

Introduction

Goodbyes are a part of life. I had to say many goodbyes to my son Mike during the time he was lost in his addiction, before he ultimately said the unfathomable goodbye.

I said goodbyes to myself, to the mom I was, to the life I led with Mike. That last goodbye has reshaped my life the most.

I can see his infamous smile and the twinkle of his baby-blue eyes as he peers over my shoulder, knowing I am honoring his request. His voice echoes in my mind: "You did it, Mom. You shared my story. I can see you've grown through the pain I left you in." I feel his presence when I write, whispering in my ear his comments, thoughts, memories, and stories of his life I'd forgotten in the aftermath of his death.

This is a story of life and death and finding new life again. I found healing for my soul in writing this journey, and I hope others reading this will too.

After high school, my son Michael struggled for four years with a heroin addiction. He plunged into a dark world that few would ever understand as he struggled with depression, anxiety, guilt, and shame. He was in and out of eight treatment centers around the country. He relocated from his birthplace in Saint Paul, Minnesota, to Carbondale, a town nestled in the mountains of Colorado. He had a total of twenty-three months of sobriety during that time.

Mike returned home after two years of living in Colorado for his eighth time in treatment. He completed his twenty-eight days and was released to a halfway house for continued recovery. On a sunny Tuesday afternoon in June 2012, I toured the facility with Mike and his dad, Allan, my husband. Two days later, two police officers came to our door and told me that my son had been found dead in a local motel. Scattered around the room was evidence of drug use. A suicide note had been left on the nightstand.

This journey through my son's addiction and then his suicide is one that no mother ever plans to undertake. I walked with Mike through his darkness and my own. Nights were filled with fear as I experienced terrifying phone calls from Mike, his friends, his counselors, and emergency rooms across the country.

Woven into this story is the golden thread of love from God, family, and friends. This stage of my journey ended in heartbreak, but I got through it because others supported me, encouraged me every step of the way, and gave me something I desperately needed: hope. With it I found the strength to persevere, and over the years it has slowly transformed me.

I wrote this book as an act of love. Reliving the last four years of my son's life has been a walk of fearlessness; in the process, I struggled but I also found a seedbed of healing. My love for Mike will never end, and it has led me out of the darkness into a place of new life. I hope to be a beacon of light for other parents who walk this same path.

As you read my story, I want you to gain a thorough understanding of addiction. I want you to realize that the person standing behind you at the grocery store, assisting you at the bank, or sitting beside you at church could be chemically dependent, and you would never know it. Maybe you've heard something through the grapevine about that lovely family living down the street struggling to get help for their addicted child. Would you judge them, thinking that something must be terribly wrong with the parents? Would you reach out? What would you say? If you don't have answers to these questions, you're not alone. Friends and family often don't know what to say or how to help people affected by addiction. I hope my story will help you help them.

Mike was not alone in his battle with heroin addiction. The number of heroin users has grown every year since 2007. According to the National Institutes of Health, in 2016 about 948,000 Americans reported using heroin in the past year. Young adults aged eighteen to twenty-five made up the largest demographic increase in use.[1]

I also hope to shed light on some of the misinformation about suicide. Considered by many in the medical field to be one of the nation's greatest health epidemics, especially among young people, it is the tenth leading cause of death among all Americans, the third leading cause of death of Americans aged ten to fourteen, and the second leading cause of death for Americans aged fifteen to thirty-four. Death by suicide is not a selfish act. A person anytime or anywhere can feel despair and hopelessness. This internal woundedness can lead to a feeling of unrelenting emotional and psychological pain, and all that person wants to do is stop the pain. Once they take that final step, that pain is gone for them. But it has been transferred to the family members, who must come to terms with an unimaginable loss.

Suicide, addiction, and depression have a very close and interconnected relationship. More than 90 percent of people who die by suicide suffered from depression or had a substance abuse disorder, or both. Depression and substance abuse combine to form a vicious cycle that all too often leads to suicide. Of all addictions, perhaps none is more likely to result in suicide than opioid addiction. Men with an opioid use disorder are twice as likely to fall victim to suicide, and women with an opioid use disorder are eight times as likely to fall victim to suicide. Opioid use is associated with an increase of 40 to 60 percent in the likelihood of suicidal thoughts and a 75 percent increase in the likelihood of attempting suicide.[2]

People with substance use disorders are about six times more likely to commit suicide than members of the general population. Substance abuse not only increases the likelihood that a person will take his or her own life but also is itself a means for committing suicide. Roughly one in three people who die from suicide are under the influence of drugs, typically alcohol or opioids such as oxycodone and heroin.[3]

Addiction and suicide left their marks on each member of our family, with devastating consequences. Though I will forever miss Mike and wish he were here, I have moved forward to live my life as fully as I can, for Mike and for myself. Now I hope that my story will encourage others who have experienced these losses.

This is not your fault. You didn't cause it. You could not have taken away the internal pain your loved one was experiencing.

I understand the swirl of emotions. I hear the pain in the telling of these stories.

You are not alone.

Part One

Part One
Part One
Part One
Part One
Part One
Part One

1. The Beginning of an Arduous Journey

June 21, 2012. When the doorbell rang, I was home doing mundane mom things: laundry, cleaning up the kitchen after breakfast, starting my to-do list, and deciding what to make for supper. I had gotten up early and already eaten breakfast, completed my morning meditations, and gone to the YMCA for a spinning class. On the way home, I'd called Mike and left him a voice message—I didn't even think about the fact he didn't answer his phone. It had been eight thirty in the morning; he was twenty-three and used to sleeping until noon. In my message, I'd asked him to give me a call when he woke up to discuss the plan we'd made the previous evening for a bike ride. It was something we often didn't have time to do, and I was excited about it. I was dying to try out the new bike helmet I'd bought the day before.

I glanced out the window as I walked to the door. Two police cruisers sat out front. I thought, *This isn't good.* A chill went down my spine, and I felt a wave of fear brush past my cheek. I hesitated before placing my hand on the doorknob. I twisted the knob and opened the door, and there stood two stoic uniformed officers.

I invited them in and asked, "Is this about Mike?"

One of the officers responded, "Yes, it is."

They followed me to the living room, where I offered them seats on the couch. I sat on our overstuffed chair to their right.

The first policeman said, "I'm sorry to inform you of the death of your son Mike."

I sucked in my breath. My stomach turned, and the blood rushed to my ears; I could see the officer's mouth moving but could not hear him. I felt I was being swept overboard into an angry, turbulent sea. As the wind and waves thundered all around me, I was sucked underwater. I felt my arms flailing and my legs kicking furiously to reach the top. It was only a few seconds, but it felt like an eternity.

The weather was unseasonably warm for June. The windows were open. Moments before, I could hear the birds singing and the neighborhood dogs barking and children's laughter somewhere nearby. The scent of lilacs turned rancid in my nostrils. Dizzy and disoriented, I tried to make sense of what the officer had just told me, but I could not.

My gaze went to the beautiful stained-glass windows in natural dark-wood frames on the stairs to our second story. They were one of the reasons we had bought this beautiful century-old home nearly twenty years ago. When my focus returned to the policemen, I could see their sad kindness waiting for me in the uncomfortable silence. In the blink of an eye my life had irreversibly changed, and I knew it would never, ever be the same.

I stammered, "Was it an overdose?"

"Yes, it appears so," the officer replied.

"Was it heroin?" I asked quietly, too overwhelmed to show what I was feeling.

"It appears likely," he said.

The officer was polite and gentle. I guessed that this was the hardest part of his job, the one he least enjoyed.

The first officer told me that Mike's body had been found by a maid at the Midway Motel in his hometown of Saint Paul, Minnesota, less than three miles from our house. The house where I had raised my youngest child, my baby boy, the child I was closest to. Needles, syringes, aluminum foil, a spoon, and other drug paraphernalia littered the room. He'd left a handwritten suicide note. The policeman addressing me had been the one to respond to the call from the motel manager. He told me the coroner had been called to the scene. Mike was now at the morgue.

Then came the one statement I've come to loathe: "I'm sorry for your loss." Not "I'm sorry about your son" or "about Mike." I didn't lose a sock or weight or my hair. *My son is dead!* exploded in my brain. *Please tell me you're sorry about him.*

Unable to acknowledge this loathsome statement, I thanked the officers, and they left. What else can I say? They did their job. What else could they have done?

I returned to the living room and sat, alone, for a minute or two to collect my thoughts. I looked down. My hands were trembling. I tried to push myself out of the chair, but my legs wouldn't hold me up. *Am I dreaming? Did they really say Mike is dead?* A shroud of darkness began to creep over me.

I took a deep breath and stood up. I was a bit wobbly,

but I walked into the kitchen and grabbed my cell phone. I looked at it, trying to think what I needed to do next. How do you move forward when you've just been told your youngest child is dead?

I remembered a time several years earlier when Mike and his two brothers, Dan and Sean, were playing a boisterous game of cops and robbers. I heard Mike yell, "Let's pretend a drive-by shooting, and I'll be the target!" At the mere thought of my sons dying, even pretend, I flew up the stairs and sat the three of them down.

"Drive-by shootings really happen, and people get killed!" I said with a stern voice.

The three of them sat there quietly, looking at their enraged mom.

"I never want you to pretend that again, ever! Do you understand?" They just nodded.

Now, standing in my kitchen, I didn't feel enraged. My heart felt broken instead.

What to do first? I called Allan, who was seventy miles away at a golf tournament. He answered his cell phone on the second or third ring.

As calmly as I could I said, "You need to come home."

There was a second of hesitation on his part.

"Why?" he asked.

I said more firmly, "You need to come home!"

"But why?" he asked a second time.

I hated to tell him his son was dead. But after thirty-six years of marriage, I knew he would not leave unless I told him.

"Allan, the police were just here. They told me Mike is dead."

"What? What do you mean, dead?"

"The policeman had just come from the motel where he'd been called. He said they found Mike in bed and next to him was a spoon and a needle and other drug paraphernalia."

"Oh God, no!"

"There was a note left on the bedside stand."

Quietly and compassionately he said, "I'll be home as soon as I can."

It was impossible for me to just sit there, waiting for Allan to come home. I jumped into my car and raced over to where Dan, Mike's eldest brother, was working. The auto repair shop where he was the head mechanic was less than two miles from the house, and it wasn't unusual for me to drop by to see him at work.

When I arrived, he was standing under a car that was hoisted up on the lift.

I hollered over to him, "Hey, Dan."

He smiled and said, "Give me a minute." This day was no different for him—yet.

I waited. When he walked over to me, I motioned him to the door. We walked outside. For a moment I couldn't speak, just stare at him, trying not to cry, and he gave me a quizzical look. Did he have an inkling of what I was about to tell him? Had he already imagined this scene playing out?

God, I hated to do this! I took a deep breath, and the

halting words spilled out of my mouth—I couldn't even string a coherent sentence together.

"Mikey's dead. The police. Just at the house. It was heroin. A note."

We stood there for several seconds, neither of us really knowing what to say. Then Dan gave me a big hug. He went inside and told his boss he needed to leave immediately. He quickly finished up what needed to be done, and then we got into our cars and drove over to the house.

I don't remember what we talked about or if we even talked at all after we arrived at the house. We paced from the kitchen to the front entryway and back into the kitchen as we waited for Allan, processing the news of Mike's death.

Dan is eight years older than Mike, who idolized him. For such a big age difference, their relationship was tight. Dan taught Mike how to fish, hunt, and drive a car. They went on campouts together. They played outdoor hockey in the winter and catch out front of the house in the summer. Dan never minded taking Mike along to his friends' houses, and his friends never minded Mike tagging along. Of course, Mike loved the attention. Dan's friends became Mike's friends, and they looked out for Mike—more than I ever realized. Soon they would surround us with the support we needed so badly.

I was standing in front of the kitchen sink, staring out the window, when movement caught my attention. Allan had walked past the window toward the backyard. I quickly walked over to open the back door. Allan saw Dan standing on the deck. I saw that Allan had already started crying. They hugged. I rushed out, and we clung to one another, chests heaving, arms locked around one another. When I finally opened my eyes to look at Dan and then Allan, their faces were streaked with tears. I let out a primal wail.

After that first wave of shared grief passed, the three of us talked about the best time to tell Sean. We knew it would be especially hard on him. Sean was only sixteen months older than Mike; it was almost like having twins. They shared everything growing up: a bedroom, clothes, friends, and secrets. They partied together and covered for each other. When they were younger, they were inseparable—if you saw one, the other was close by. One time, when Mike was four or five years old, he walked over to visit Mr. Bucher, our elderly neighbor who loved seeing the boys and always had homemade cookies in his cookie jar. When I walked over to get Mike, Mr. B said, "Bye, Sean," and I immediately reminded him that it was Mike, not Sean. Mike, not missing a beat, said, "Sean or Mike, doesn't really matter," and then skipped off toward home. I still smile thinking of that memory. Looking back, I realize Mike was comfortable with who he was. He didn't care if people confused him with Sean, which happened frequently throughout their early years. Mike was confident.

Dan, Allan, and I decided to drive to Hastings, Minnesota, forty miles south of the Twin Cities, to meet Sean at work. He was very surprised to see us walk into the Verizon store he managed.

"Hi, Sean," I said, trying to keep emotion from my voice. "Can we talk to you in private?"

"Sure, let's step out into the hallway." Sean motioned us to the door behind the counter.

Allan, Dan, and I surrounded Sean. He seemed perplexed.

"Sean"—Allan's voice cracked—"Mike's dead. It was an overdose."

The silence was deafening.

Then Sean's arms opened wide, and the four of us huddled together. I could feel Sean's shoulders shaking as he wrapped his arm tighter around my shoulder.

"Dad, will you pray?"

It was a question I didn't expect. We pulled ourselves a few steps closer yet and bowed our heads in that deserted hallway.

"Lord, we need you right now. Help us, please, help us," Allan pleaded ever so quietly. "We don't know what to do or say. Give us the strength we need. Comfort us. Be with us. Amen."

I hugged Sean one more time before he walked back into the store to tell his boss that he had a family emergency and needed to leave immediately. Within minutes we were heading home again.

Dan returned with Sean, and Allan and I drove back in our car. I don't remember much about the trip home, but we talked about the things we would need to do next. I took out a notepad I kept in the console and made notes. There were people we needed to tell: our family, friends, neighbors. I called Pastor Nate from our church to tell him. He prayed for us over the phone. Later that evening, he and his wife, Miriam, would come to see us. The four of us sat on our back deck as they helped us make preliminary plans for Mike's visitation and funeral.

Many church friends called to give their condolences and ask what they could do to help us. But in those first twenty-four hours, the shock and numbness of learning about Mike's death made answering such questions impossible.

Allan and I stopped by the Ramsey County Medical Examiner's Office before going home. We had to wait several minutes before the medical examiner was available. It was an eerie feeling as we sat in the waiting room. I remember it vividly. We sat in uncomfortable chairs. The assistant sat at a wooden desk, working on her computer. There were a couple of drooping plants badly in need of water, and the lighting was subdued. It felt like the air had been sucked out of the room by an invisible vacuum cleaner. It was deathly quiet. I thought, *This can't be happening to us.*

At last, the medical examiner escorted us back to his office. He told us what he knew after seeing Mike's body: Mike looked healthy, and his skin was smooth and clear. He didn't see any bruises. There was a single injection site on Mike's right forearm that had been covered with a bandage. He would do an autopsy and a toxicology screen; we would receive the results in a few weeks.

When the results came in the mail several weeks later, there wasn't anything out of the ordinary, beyond what we already knew: Mike was a healthy twenty-three-year-old with a history of chemical dependency. A white substance and other drug paraphernalia had been found in the motel room, along with a note. A small puncture mark in the elbow pit revealed a small amount of blood present in the subcutaneous tissue. The drugs found in his system indicated heroin toxicity.

I really wanted to see Mike's body while we were there, but the medical examiner said he thought it would be better for us to wait to see him at the funeral home. Reluctantly, I agreed. Then he handed me a brown paper bag containing Mike's belongings. For a second time that day I was told, "I'm so sorry for your loss." Then he walked us to the front door. All I could muster was a weak thank you as we left. I could feel the bright sun's heat on my face. I looked around the parking lot; just a few cars were parked there. What did I expect, a parking lot full of cars?

The paper bag in my hands contained Mike's clothes, wallet, and car keys along with a small manila envelope holding loose change and a copy of his suicide note. I hugged it close to my heart. I got into the car, opened the bag, and took a deep breath. The contents smelled like Mikey. I crumpled forward in my seat as sobs escaped my lips. The reality of what had happened was only beginning to settle in. A wave of nausea hit me as I tried to catch my breath, but my tears continued to flow.

We drove back to our house in silence, lost in our thoughts. As the door closed behind us, I was desperately trying to shut out the fact we now had two sons, not three. Dan and Sean arrived a few minutes later, and we began making the saddest phone calls of our lives.

When you receive that call and hear "Are you sitting down? I have something to tell you," the weight of those words drops into the pit of your stomach. Making that call, explaining it over and over, was a million times more heart wrenching. The stunned silence on the other end feels so surreal, almost movie-like. But it was real. I heard myself saying the words; their intensity was undeniable. But delivering that blow again and again was numbing.

After dinner that evening, the four of us drove to the Midway Motel to retrieve Mike's car. While we were standing in the parking lot, the woman who owned the motel walked up to me and gently placed her hands on either side of my face. Patting my cheeks, she said in her broken English, "Why? Why would he do that? He was such a beautiful boy."

I looked into her eyes, but I had no words. I shrugged my shoulders and shook my head.

She asked if I wanted to see the room. I hesitated, and she told me it had been cleaned up. I agreed.

We all walked the few feet to the room and stepped inside. It seemed so sterile: walls painted a light color, the barest of furnishings. With the drapes pulled closed, it felt impersonal—just what you would expect in an inexpensive motel room. I looked at the bed, now made up fresh, and imagined Mike leaning against the headboard. I felt a stab of pain in my chest at the thought that my son had ended his life in this stark, gloomy room—alone.

That visual would haunt me for weeks. Then, one morning, as I played that scene in my mind once more, I had a vision of Mike on that bed but leaning back against his Heavenly Father, whose arms were wrapped around my son. God wept with Mike as my son injected that lethal dose of heroin into his vein. He held Mike tightly through the peaceful transition from life to death. As the vision faded, I felt at peace knowing that Mike was not alone that evening.

We had one final task to do. We returned home, where Dan and Sean sat on the living-room couch the two policemen had occupied earlier that day, and I sat on the same overstuffed chair. Allan took the chair next to me. He poured out the contents of the manila envelope from the medical examiner on the coffee table. He picked up the note and read it silently; he passed it to me to read, and I passed it to Dan, who passed it Sean. We sat there together, processing the note. There were no words, just tears. The note read,

> To my beloved family, I love you guys so damn much. I am filled with so much pain, sorrow, insecurity, but mostly shame and guilt. This is the most selfish thing a person can do. As a child growing up, I never thought my life would ever turn into this. It's almost impossible for me to think anything positive about myself after the things I have done. It feels that these things are insurmountable for me to get over. The chatter in my head it too much, telling me I'm not good enough, I am not worthy of the wonderful, amazing, unconditional love that is shown me on a daily basis. I lived life to the fullest, experienced so many heart-touching moments and lived in a world of love from you. This addiction is so strong and never lets up. Over the past four years I have put the people in my life in so much pain. I carry that pain with me and cannot process it or let it go. I just can't keep doing this to myself or my family. I had the most amazing childhood, having two loving parents, two older brothers who always looked

out for me and showed me how to live life. I love you more than you all know. Don't stop being yourselves . . .

Mike, my son, my baby boy, gone forever. There would be no more calls from him, no more bike rides, and no more seeing him at family celebrations. Hardest of all, I would never hold him or kiss him again or tell him "I love you," and that thought ripped my heart into shreds.

I was overwhelmed with questions. How did this happen? What brought Mike to this place of hopelessness, with only one option left?

I want to take you back to the summer of 2008, when this long and arduous journey began. It has brought me great pain and sorrow, hurt and anger, but most importantly, hope.

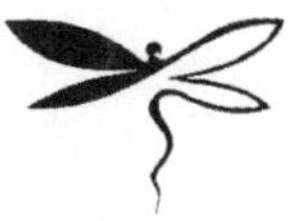

2. A Gut-Wrenching Experience

In mid-June 2008, four sons and four dads planned a five-day Boundary Waters Canoe Area (BWCA) camping trip: Andy and Jim, Greg and Tom, Anthony and Jim, and Mike and his dad. Mike and his friends had gone to junior high and high school together, and they all liked sports: hockey, soccer, baseball, and basketball. They had a common interest in camping and fishing, plus they really enjoyed hanging out together.

During spring break the previous year, they'd rented a yurt—a circular, domed tent—on a frozen lake just off the Gunflint Trail for two nights of camping. Anthony recalled, "The four of us drove up north and met the owner of a B and B who rented us the yurt. He had us throw our things on a sled, which he pulled behind his snowmobile. We walked a mile and a half to a remote location on the lake. As he pulled our belongings through a foot and a half of snow and slush, we talked among ourselves about whether or not our things would make it to the yurt dry. (By the way, they did.) The yurt was heated by a wood stove; unfortunately, we didn't listen to the owner's instructions on how to use it. Our first morning we woke up to no heat, and frost had coated everything inside. After we ate breakfast, we planned to ice fish. I remember the owner had warned us to check the thickness of the ice on the lake before we set out fishing because there were areas where the ice wasn't thick or safe enough to walk on. Again, we didn't really listen carefully to his instructions. Of course, Mike was the first one out on the lake to fish. He just drilled a hole in the ice, put his line in, and then promptly fell through the hole, up to his waist in ice-cold water. Oh my gosh, we laughed so hard as Mike pulled himself out of the water."

They were all excited for this next adventure. The BWCA is a protected wilderness where visitors can explore thousands of miles of canoe routes over more than a thousand lakes and streams. It's famous for walleye, northern pike, and smallmouth bass fishing, as well as sightings of loons, eagles, moose, deer, black bears, and other wildlife.[4] Considered by some to be the most beautiful wilderness ever, the BWCA experience is entirely rustic: no motors, no electricity, no cell-phone towers or telephone lines, and no roads to the inner lakes. The BWCA draws people who want to challenge themselves. You must carry all your own equipment, including a tent, sleeping bag, camp stove, food, and few extras, usually in a large canvas backpack that can weigh as much as seventy pounds, and leave no trace of your passage. Travelers cover long stretches in canoes, but to get from one lake to another, you walk, loaded down, as you portage (carry the canoe overhead over land between the lakes and ponds). Then you load up the canoes again and paddle through the lakes to your campsite.

The group left late on a Thursday evening to make the five-hour drive to the BWCA. They arrived at the campground in the wee hours of the morning and planned to sleep around a fire pit until the sun came up. After everyone turned in for the night, Allan got up to relieve himself, and as he returned, he observed Mike in the back of the van with a lighter and aluminum foil; he appeared to be inhaling something. Allan said nothing but wondered what Mike was doing. As morning came and the group prepared their canoes, Allan opted not to confront Mike on what he'd seen just a few hours earlier.

The group entered the BWCA and paddled to their campsite. It was the first time this group of guys had all gone camping together. They fished, hiked, canoed, and jumped off of cliffs into the lakes. In the evenings, they hung around the campfire, cooking dinner, talking, and joking with one another. Everything seemed to be going great for everyone except for Mike. He wasn't his usual fun and outgoing self. He isolated himself in the tent and slept a lot, and the few times he joined the group's activities, he participated very little. This was odd behavior for someone who was normally in the middle of everything and the center of attention.

Andy, Greg, and Anthony were Mike's closest friends, and they noticed this change and asked him what was going on. Mike explained that he was very tired from working full time at his job, in which he ripped out and replaced carpet, tile, and linoleum in residential and commercial buildings. His friends accepted his explanation.

However, after returning from the trip, Allan's first call was to Dan, explaining what he had seen on the camping trip.

"Dad," Dan replied, "a week or so before your trip, Sean

called me after a mutual friend told him that Mike was using drugs. I didn't say anything to you when you were getting ready for the trip."

"I wish you would have told me. I've been so worried about Mike, not knowing what was going on."

"Dad, I am sorry. I confronted Mike myself after I talked to Sean. Mike vehemently denied he was doing drugs. I believed him."

"I get that," Allan replied. "What do we do now? I haven't said anything to Mom yet."

"I will make a few calls. I will try to get to the bottom of this."

"Okay, call me as soon as you find something out."

"I will, Dad. Love you."

Dan called Allan back a couple days later and said, "I did some checking around. I'm having a really hard time believing this, but I think it might be heroin. What are we going to do?"

"I sure don't know right now. Give me some time to think about it. I know I need to tell Mom tonight. She'll be so upset. We'll go from there, okay?"

"Yeah, that sounds like a plan."

That evening, Allan walked into the kitchen as I was finishing up the supper dishes and sat down at the kitchen table.

"Linda, I need to talk to you about something."

He had a serious look on his face and a tone of voice that was completely unfamiliar. I immediately sat down in the chair across from him, saying, "Okay, it sounds serious."

"I have something I need to tell you about that happened when Mike and I were on our BWCA trip."

"Oh, okay. What is it?" I thought maybe one of the guys in the group had gotten hurt or something, but then he explained what he had seen and what Dan had said.

"Heroin?" I asked. "What the heck? Are you sure?"

"That's what Dan thinks at this point."

I couldn't wrap my head around this. *Mike using drugs! And heroin, of all things. Oh my God!* Needless to say, I was thoroughly caught off guard. Never in my wildest dreams would I have suspected he would use any drugs, let alone something as dangerous as heroin. I remembered in my high school years that kids using drugs, especially heroin, were labeled losers. Mike was no loser! He had the whole package: intelligence, good looks, an incredible sense of humor, an outgoing personality, and no fear of taking risks. I would soon learn just how many of those struggling with substance abuse have so many of these attributes. Now, though, I just sat there, staring into space as I tried to process this information.

On Friday evening, a week after the BWCA trip, Allan and I called a family meeting. In our home, family meetings were common and mandatory. Any of the five of us could call one whenever something important was going on in our lives that needed family input. We knew Mike would be there for it.

The five of us sat on our back deck. We all were a little on edge as the meeting began. Allan started off by saying this was for and about Mike, and that we suspected he was using drugs. As I looked around the table, Allan looked the most notably shaken. I could see the fear and anxiety etched in his face. Dan was pensive. We had said nothing to Sean about Mike's drug use because we were afraid that Sean might say something to Mike and Mike would avoid the meeting. Looking back, I know that was a mistake, one of many we made during this journey. Sitting in his chair on the deck, Sean had that deer-in-the-headlights look. I just felt numb inside.

Allan said a short prayer. Then we went around the table affirming Mike. We told him how much we loved him, how much potential he had, and how our lives would be tragically different if anything happened to him. I think he already knew this. Allan and I tried to instill in each of our sons an understanding of how much they were loved, how valuable their lives were, and that they could do anything they set out to do. Each one of us went over to Mike to hug him. At that point everyone started to cry. I suspect Mike knew what was coming next. Allan confronted Mike with what he'd seen in the BWCA.

It was quiet as we waited for him to respond. To his everlasting credit, Mike looked around the table at each one of us and then admitted he was using drugs. He told us it was heroin. He was smoking it and not injecting it. He didn't lie about it; there was no deception or denial. He said he wanted to stop using and didn't think he could do it on his own.

I sat back in my chair watching my guys, these four physically and emotionally strong men, reduced to tears in this gut-wrenching moment. We hugged and cried, especially Mike, who sobbed and sobbed. I think it was a huge relief to him to have this out in the open. And we were at a loss as to where to begin, now that Mike had just admitted to what we would soon learn was a heroin addiction.

Dan told Mike that he needed to remove any problematic numbers from his cell phone, namely his drug dealers and any of his friends who used illicit drugs regularly. Mike removed those phone numbers immediately. Then we sat there for a while, our minds a jumble of thoughts on what the next possible steps might be. All of us felt drained.

Shortly after our discussion ended, Mike made the brave step of owning his addiction. He began calling and texting his friends to tell them about his drug use. Most were very surprised at his admission, but within thirty minutes two carloads of Mike's friends showed up at the house, including his best friend, Greg. They met downstairs for a long time as Mike told them about his drug use. I don't know what he said, but at one point I could hear sobs coming from the basement. Greg came to talk to me and offer whatever help he could. He said he felt really helpless; he was heading away to college the next week and wouldn't be around to support us.

Meanwhile, my mind was in overdrive. What kind of help did Mike need? Did he need treatment at a center? How do you go about finding a treatment center on a Friday night? Who do you talk to about this? How would this affect our family? Would Dan and Sean support their brother? What could Allan and I do? What would our families think? Did I miss warning signs of drug use? Was any of this my fault? Would my marriage survive this ordeal?

Over the following weeks and months, we would find the answers together.

3. A Mind Plagued with Anxiety

Mike was our "surprise" baby. We thought our family was complete with Dan and Sean. Then I found out I was pregnant.

I left a card on the dining room table for Allan to open when he arrived home from work. When he opened the card, he read, *Life is full of surprises. One became two, we thought we were through. But that's not quite true. Here is to you and me and number THREE.* To say he was very surprised was an understatement. After the shock wore off, he was very excited.

Mike was born by cesarean section at 9:28 a.m., 8 hours and 88 minutes into 8/8/88. (I chose August 8 because it was my dad's birthday.) Mike had a perfectly round head, not the cone shape Dan and Sean had from their trips through the birth canal. He had tons of very light blond hair and gray-blue eyes that turned vibrant blue a few days after birth. He was a beautiful baby and a joy to our family from the very beginning.

The summer when Mike was four, I took him and Sean to one of Dan's baseball games. After the game, as I loaded the kids in the car, I asked Mike what he and Sean had done during the game. He quipped, "Well, we didn't look at magazines with naked women in them."

"Why not?" I asked, smiling to myself.

"Because John's mom took them away from us." He sounded quite annoyed.

Sean, older and worldly at age five, leaned over and whispered to Mike, "We're not supposed to tell Mom about that!"

When Mike was four or five, he began placing his pillow in the refrigerator. When I inquired as to why, he told me, "I like to lay my cheek on a cool pillow." Every day for several weeks, he placed his pillow in the fridge every morning. Then, at bedtime, just as I began reading him and Sean a bedtime story, he'd say, "Stop! I have to get my pillow!" Then he'd jump out of his bed and leap the stairs two at a time to retrieve it. Even when he was an adult, he still liked a cool pillow, although I don't think he put it in the fridge. He told me once that he wanted to develop a type of a pillow that stayed cool. He said he would call it the Chill-O Pillow.

Mike seemed to grow up fast, as younger children often do. He had Dan and Sean to teach him. He attended Randolph Heights Elementary School with Sean. When Mike was in kindergarten, I worked in the school office part time. One afternoon his teacher, Mrs. Thomas, walked into the office and expressed to me her displeasure at his latest antic. The children had been discussing Santa Claus, and Mike casually informed them that there was no Santa: it was their parents. To her horror, she had to come up with an instant explanation that would satisfy the kids and keep the parents happy. Now, on her break, she asked me to please explain to Mike that it was not okay to share about who Santa was or wasn't. I secretly thought it was hilarious but told her I would do that.

Another time, Mikey walked into the office of the school principal, Bill Sheppard, sat in the closest chair, and said, "Hi, Bill, how's it going?" They had a pleasant conversation, but after Mike left, Bill chided me. He wanted me to tell Mike to address him as Mr. Sheppard. Then the two of us had a good laugh over it.

One afternoon I took Mike to Target with me, and the cashier took one look at his eyes and asked, "Where did you get those beautiful blue eyes?" Mike very nonchalantly stated, "From Tawget"; everyone within hearing distance laughed.

Then there was the time Mike and Sean made a campfire in the garage with sticks, newspaper, and a lighter. They were so proud when they showed it to me. Another time, I heard the water spigot turn on when the two of them were in the backyard. After a few minutes I heard their unbridled laughter. I walked outside and saw, first, their clothes, neatly folded on the picnic table, and then, around the corner, a homegrown Slip 'N Slide. The grass had been turned into a large, muddy lake, and the boys were running and sliding on their stomachs headfirst through it—*naked*. I laughed as they ran and slid over and over until they were completely covered in mud and all I could see was the sparkle in their eyes. I had such fun hosing them off after they finished.

As the three boys got older, their games became a bit more sophisticated. They spent hours in the basement playing Rollerblade hockey. From the kitchen I could hear them taking slap shots on goalie Dan Morrison and announcing each goal they made, just like in a professional game: "And scoring for the Wild, Mikey Morrison, number fourteen, his first hat trick" or "A two-minute penalty on Sean Morrison, number twenty-two, for tripping." Those times were precious to me. Our home was in constant motion. They roughhoused with one another, wrestling like on *WWE Raw* with the Rock. My living room was a den of boy activities as they ran and jumped on the furniture, threw fastballs to one another, and hit plastic hockey pucks with shortened sticks. Several lamps bit the dust during their games.

Mike's sense of humor was notorious, and sometimes it took the whole family with it. Allan noted, "Mike couldn't stand people who made noises while eating. Smacking their lips or slurping a glass of milk at the dinner table usually resulted in Mike responding with an exaggerated sound level. As kids usual with kids, this only aggravated the initial offender, who responded in a similarly exaggerated way, on many occasions resulting in a dinner table that sounded more like a zoo than a home." But Mike also had a sensitive side, and he felt things very deeply. Allan recalled, "When Linda's mom died in 2006, we called Mike to tell him. He went to the nursing home and sat with her body. The nurse told Linda that she could hear him sobbing from down the hall. He was all heart."

What we didn't have words for at the time was Mike's anxiety, which was especially strong in social settings. Looking back, I realize it affected him as early as second grade, when Mike would tell me he didn't like school and wanted to stay home. It was a struggle to get him to school most days, but at first, I dismissed these symptoms as a kid not wanting to attend class. When it didn't go away, though, I went to see his teacher. She said that Mike seemed fine. I didn't believe her, so I talked to some other parents of Mike's classmates, and they offered me a different story: his teacher used shame tactics that damaged his self-esteem and desire to go to school.

I encouraged Mike each day to be positive and do his best. His anxiety got worse over time, but he managed to complete his elementary years by learning to hide it from everyone—especially from me. Therefore, I believed he had overcome it.

In junior high his coping skills continued to diminish. He didn't receive the credits he needed to pass ninth grade because he'd missed so many classes and had so many incomplete assignments and failing test scores. He was passed on to tenth grade with the understanding that he would make up the credits he lacked before he graduated.

In high school his anxiety became more acute. He had panic attacks that caused his heart to race and his palms to sweat when he had to take tests or participate in class discussions. Some days, just being at school was physically and emotionally distressing for him. Many days, he drove himself to school, got halfway there, and turned around to come home or meet up with friends skipping school. Mike usually called me when he couldn't make himself get to classes. I began to worry that he might not be able to graduate with his class.

In the spring of Mike's senior year, Allan and I spent time and money on getting him ready to graduate. I hired tutors to help him complete his math and English requirements. I also spent many nights helping him with his homework—well, actually, doing it for him. When he walked the graduation line, I felt I had graduated too.

The summer after graduation, Mike started to really connect with his dad as an adult. In Mike's eulogy, Allan recalled,

> Mike was wise beyond his years. He was intuitive and discerning. I loved the talks we had. This was epitomized by what Mike and I came fondly to refer to as the Bike Ride. I loved having discussions with Mike about God, life, our purpose, our dreams, and on and on. In the summer after his high school graduation, Mike and I ended up on a long ride on the Midtown Greenway bike trail that runs through Minneapolis. That single ride became a legend to Mike and me. On that ride, we discussed life, his future plans, how to get there, what to watch out for. And as we had these same discussions over the next few years, we always smiled and referred back to the Bike Ride where the discussions all started. I loved Mike for the times we would just talk and talk and talk about important stuff in our lives.

It's bittersweet to see your youngest kid taking those steps into adulthood. What we didn't know at the time was that his addiction had already taken root.

After Mike entered his first treatment center, I learned that he had started self-medicating with narcotic pain pills after he had his wisdom teeth pulled in high school. I didn't realize at the time that the euphoric effects the pain meds had on his brain, the feelings of well-being and elation, were a turning point for him. I think they helped him cover up his feelings of anxiety.

He moved on to other drugs, including oxycodone, Vicodin, Percocet, and Adderall, a drug used to treat attention deficit hyperactivity disorder. I wasn't sure how he had gotten the drugs—maybe from classmates—but I knew it wasn't hard to get them. I was naïve about the addictive properties of such drugs and had no idea that they became an ongoing problem for him. Mike told us these drugs had helped decrease his anxiety and helped him feel "normal."

4. Chemical Addiction: A Strange New World

On Saturday morning, I called Mike's health insurance company to see if insurance would pay for treatment. I found out that a weekend is not a good time to contact them.

On Monday morning, I called Blue Cross Blue Shield and talked to a representative to find out what options were available on Mike's personal health insurance. (This was before a child of eighteen and not in college could stay on their parents' plan.) The agent told me that Mike had behavioral health coverage on his plan, and I remembered that when Mike was looking for health insurance, he'd asked me if I knew what behavioral health was. I didn't know, but he told me he would add it to his coverage.

Behavioral health and mental health are closely related and contribute to an individual's overall health. Mental health refers to how well one copes with stress and continues to function in their daily life. Depression and anxiety fall under mental health disorders that can disrupt one's daily life. Behavioral health is the link between one's behaviors and overall well-being, behaviors that can be changed and a more hopeful concept for those individuals who experience mental illness or addiction, and can be less stigmatizing. A multidisciplinary approach can include services provided by social workers, counselors, psychiatrists, and physicians that encompass prevention, intervention, treatment, and recovery support.

The agent informed me of the different treatment centers available on Mike's plan. Our first choice, Hazelden, was on that list. Now the Hazelden Betty Ford Foundation, this internationally renowned drug and alcohol treatment center is headquartered in Center City, Minnesota, less than an hour's drive from our home.

I called them next and explained Mike's situation. They said they'd need to call the insurer for qualification purposes and would get back to us. We found out later that afternoon that Mike qualified for Hazelden but because of his issues with anxiety and payments Blue Cross had previously made, we would need to pay the $28,000 cost of the twenty-eight-day treatment upfront while his insurance company sorted out what would be covered. So we maxed out all our credit cards in order to pay for Mike's first treatment. Allan and I told Mike that any costs incurred not covered by insurance would come from his college fund. Mike agreed.

On Tuesday morning, July 29, four days after our family intervention, Allan and I drove Mike to Hazelden. His first meeting there was a chemical dependency evaluation, a typical initial step to determine whether treatment is right for a person. It is administered by a qualified, licensed alcohol and drug addiction counselor. If the evaluation determined that Mike did need treatment, he wanted to be admitted to their Plymouth facility, a center for youth under twenty-one.

The counselor spent several hours with Mike, completing a written record of his personal information, including a medical and sociodemographic history—his age, gender, education, marital status, occupation, income, family size, and other data. Then they went over his written information together. During this interview, Mike shared his concerns about his chemical dependency that I believe he had kept to himself until that day. Next, the counselor spoke to Allan and me about what we knew of Mike's drug use. After reviewing all the information, she recommended inpatient treatment for Mike and made arrangements to have him admitted at the Plymouth site. A bed would be available early afternoon, and we would need to drive Mike there.

On the way over, we stopped for lunch at Trapper's Family Restaurant, which has since closed, in Lindstrom. Mike was starving. He ordered a double cheeseburger, a large order of fries, and a strawberry shake. We talked about his next steps. Mike was very upbeat and ready for treatment. Allan and I felt apprehensive as we drove him there, but we were glad he was going.

Later that afternoon, Mike, with his suitcase in hand, entered his first inpatient treatment center. It turned out to be a very exhausting day for the three of us. Still, we were relieved. We knew he was in a great place, getting the help he needed—and we knew he was safe.

Mike spent his first four or five days in the detoxification unit, a medical unit with staff trained to aid the patients as they withdraw from drugs and/or alcohol. The effects of coming off heroin are quite uncomfortable but usually not life threatening. Mike experienced restlessness and sleeplessness. He had sweats and chills and felt tired and lethargic. He told me the staff gave him trazodone to help him sleep. In addition to the physical discomfort of heroin withdrawal, an individual might experience a number of mental health issues as well, such as depression, anxiety, suicidal ideation, mood swings, and irritability.[5] Mike told me he experienced mild depression and mood swings and felt very irritable. He was given Subutex/Suboxone, a medication to help curb the cravings during withdrawal. Mike tolerated the medication very well with few side effects.

After his time in detox, he moved to the unit where he would spend his remaining twenty-eight days. One day would go well there, and then the next day he would struggle to want to stay in treatment. He was still craving heroin and trying to come to terms with his addiction. This can be a struggle for anyone in the early stages of change in the treatment setting.

At one point, Mike's counselor, Noelle, commented to us that she'd never seen an addiction as strong as Mike's in someone that young. He would call us and tell us that he wanted to leave the program and use. We'd talk him into staying, and he'd stay a day or two more, and then he'd call again to tell us he was leaving. It was a daily battle for him and us: yes, he wanted to stop using—yes, he knew his drug of choice could kill him—yet he still wanted to leave and use.

On Friday, August 1, I flew to Denver, Colorado, for a week to be with my dad and stepmom. They were attending a Korean War ex-POW conference. My dad had been a POW for most of the Korean War, and I had been very excited to join them, but in light of what had been happening with Mike, the trip had lost its appeal. Still, it had been planned for months, and Allan felt it was important that I go. I went, and I'm glad I did; I had a great time, even though thoughts of Mike filled my mind throughout my visit. The three of us talked a lot about Mike and his addiction, which had taken them by surprise. They took it very hard, especially my dad, who was especially close to Mike.

I flew back August 7 on an evening flight. It was good to be home. As Allan and I talked about my trip, Mike called. He told me he had broken a couple rules. Residential treatment centers have set rules and regulations that help clients succeed while creating a stable living space where they feel safe and protected from the temptation to use, and clients must follow them to stay in the program. Mike said he'd explain what happened later, after he had talked to Noelle, who was waiting for him in her office. The high anxiety I felt mounted as we waited for Mike to call back.

You never know what's coming next when you're waiting for a call from a person with a substance use disorder. I have learned that this is a common experience among those with a loved one in treatment. You think everything is going according to plan, that everything is going to work out, and then, out of the blue, BAM! Something unexpected happens. Perhaps the person relapses or decides to leave treatment or they break a rule at the center. You find yourself on edge, waiting for the other shoe to drop. And it usually does.

When the phone rang later that evening, it was Noelle. She explained that Mike wasn't doing his assignments. In the program, part of the day is spent in educational lectures about addiction, its impact on your life, and what changes you need to make. It is followed by a time to process the lecture with a peer group. People in treatment get daily written assignments that follow the Twelve Steps of Alcoholics Anonymous (see the back of this book). AA is an international fellowship of people who have had a drinking problem. It is nonprofessional, self-supporting, multiracial, apolitical, and available almost everywhere. Membership is open to anyone who wants to do something about their drinking problem. People facing addiction help one another abstain from drinking and sustain sobriety.[6] Time in treatment is also set aside for people to reflect on what they are learning about themselves.

Mike was arriving late to group or making excuses about why his assignments weren't done. Noelle told us that he had plenty of time to complete them and there was no excuse for not having them done. Mike wasn't using his time wisely. In addition, Mike had been fraternizing with the female patients, which is against the rules, and he had been warned about it already. Clients go through a program to focus on themselves and get help for their substance use, not to get romantically involved. Doing so can be disruptive to the group and a distraction for the individuals. And, we knew, Mike was easily distracted by the chance to flirt with women.

At the Plymouth center, young men and women live separately and mix only in group lectures. Each group walks to meals and lectures together. They can say hi as they pass each other but nothing more. However, Mike was finding ways to spend time with some of the women. If this continued, he could be discharged from the program. We certainly didn't want that to happen.

Noelle told us that Mike had taken responsibility for his infractions and had come to her first about them. The three of us talked about his progress; he was about where they expected him to be at this point. Noelle said he was having problems opening up to his peer group about his feelings and emotions. I got the feeling that this step made Mike feel vulnerable. He was fearful about how others perceived him. He wanted to be the macho, badass heroin addict. Discussing his feelings took him out of his comfort zone. She said he had made some progress, though, and was starting to understand some of the origins of his use of drugs. I took that as a good sign.

The next day was Mike's twentieth birthday. His counselor suggested I bring a cake to celebrate. We discussed that it might be hard for him to spend his birthday in treatment. I bought a birthday cake, a card, balloons, and some cookies and candy for him. I drove out to the center to drop off everything. I was hoping I'd be able to see him and wish him a happy birthday, but he was in a group session. I left everything I'd brought with the people at the front desk.

Driving home, it hit me hard: I was not only sad about Mike being in treatment on his birthday but also angry with him because he had chosen to use drugs and now was putting our family though this ordeal. Birthdays in our family are very special. Even if we don't see one another, we still call to give our love and best wishes. I felt deprived because I wasn't able to see or talk to him, hug him, or wish him a happy birthday in person.

I realized I was grieving. I was grieving the loss of my child—the person he had been before using—and all the hopes and dreams I had for him. This was not how I'd imagined his life or mine turning out. Hot tears of anger flowed down my cheeks. I pulled over at the nearest rest stop, turned off the engine, and pounded the steering wheel as hard as I could with both hands, yelling, "Why?! Why is this happening to me?!" Anger surged through me; I was mad at the lack of control in my life and mad at myself for reacting to it. Would my life ever be the same again?

He called later that night, and he'd been crying. Noelle had been right; it was hard on Mike to be in treatment on his birthday. He thanked me for bringing the sweets, balloons, and card. I listened to him describe his day, how he was struggling with sharing his feelings and emotions with his peer group, as Noelle had told us. He said he didn't know his peers and didn't trust them. But Mike acknowledged that this was where he needed to be and that he had to do this work, even though it "sucked." He wasn't talking about leaving. That was a good sign.

On Sunday, August 10, two days after his birthday, we had our first visit with Mike at Hazelden. I was very stressed and anxious about the visit. I baked chocolate chip cookies and packed up the personal items that Mike hadn't thought to take with him: a few pairs of socks, mouthwash, hand lotion, his workout clothes, and cash.

When we arrived, all the items we brought were searched. I thought that was weird. Who would bring drugs into the treatment center? I found out they were looking for items containing alcohol, such as mouthwash, toothpaste, and even hand lotion. Everything had to be alcohol-free. It felt like I was visiting a prisoner. We had to sign in and have our bags searched. The staff called to Mike's unit to inform him he had visitors.

Several minutes later, he walked through the doors. It was so good to see him. I cried as he hugged me. I could feel his heart beating as fast as mine. He looked good. He'd put on some weight, his eyes were clear and bright, and a smile lit up his face, something I hadn't seen for a while. He took the bags we'd brought and thanked us for bringing them. Then he showed us around the center. We saw the room he shared with another patient, where he ate meals, the group meeting rooms, and the workout room, and he introduced us to the guys he'd met there. My anxiety lessened as I saw where he was living and a smile on his face again.

He talked a lot about himself and all he had learned in the past couple weeks. He definitely had his struggles, but he was working on them. As the recovery mantra says, "One day at a time." He talked about his aftercare plan and what he felt he needed to do. We encouraged him to work on taking care of himself and healing before worrying about his aftercare. He talked through the entire two-hour visit. All too quickly we had to leave, but we felt good about the progress we saw in Mike.

As we headed home, I said, "I thought the visit went well, Allan. What did you think?"

"Mike looks really good. Boy, he sure seems to be absorbing this Twelve-Step stuff."

"I know, I could hardly get a word in edgewise. I think he's in the right place. I'm so surprised at how many older men seem so drawn to him. They all seem to really like him. Mikey sure has the gift of gab."

"He does. I hope he's doing more than gabbing while he's in here, though."

"Yeah, me too. Only time will tell."

That night I wrote in my journal,

> God is good. He is working in and through all of us in this situation. I see how I stress about things I have no control over, and those things are totally in God's care and timing. I praise God for the good and the hard times, and I pray He continues to work in Mike. It's hard to watch Mike go through this. I feel so helpless to help him. I know in my mind I can't help him; he has to do this himself. But I'm a fixer and I want to fix this. I have to give him to God so that God can do His work in Mike.

We didn't hear from Mike on Monday. That usually meant he was doing group activities or was having a hard day. On those hard days he didn't like calling. I knew that the treatment program kept patients very busy, and I thought things were going well for him.

Early Tuesday evening, exactly two weeks after Mike was admitted to Hazelden, he called me. He told me that the previous week he and some other patients had been huffing—inhaling a chemical vapor to attain a high.[6] The effect may be similar to alcohol intoxication. You can get this high from a wide variety of common household substances, such as hair-care products, deodorant, nail polish, felt-tip markers, or computer-cleaning spray. The first time Mike was confronted by Noelle, he denied it. But one of the other patients told Mike's counselor that he had been involved, and Mike was confronted a second time and admitted to it. This infraction, Mike told me, could lead to his dismissal.

He said he had talked at length with Noelle about what happened. She told him she would go to bat for him to try to keep him in the program but beyond that it was out of her hands. I sensed some remorse in Mike as we talked. He acknowledged that he needed to be there, needed help, and that if he was not able to stay, there was a great chance that he would go back to drugs. In Mike's own words, "That could end my life." I was stunned by those words. I couldn't think about this challenge ending badly for him. I just wanted my Mikey back, whole and healthy. And my life back to the way it was before drugs entered our lives.

Didn't he know what could happen if he was discharged early? I was afraid he would return to using because he didn't have the understanding or tools that would help him stay clean and sober. I found out later in our journey that if he returned to using the same amount as before, he could overdose and possibly die.

My gaze jumped between objects as I worried where he would go and what he would do. I felt this was no surprise to God; He knew this would happen. I'd been praying for God's will to be done. In my heart I sincerely hoped Mike would get a second chance. If not, then God had a different plan for him. I called friends and family and our church prayer team and sent out emails. I explained the situation and asked for prayers. I was torn between asking them to pray for God's will and for Mike to be able to stay. I wanted to be faithful to God's will, but I didn't want my son to go back to using or to leave treatment.

Mike called back later in the evening. He sounded pretty bummed out, but he thanked me for talking to him earlier. I asked about the rules regarding his possible dismissal, and he said it was on an individual basis. We both hoped he could stay. I told him I was praying for him, as were many others, and he said he appreciated that. Then I gave the phone to Allan. Whenever Mike felt guilt, shame, or remorse, he did not want to talk to his dad. Allan was the one who asked the hard questions of Mike, which usually pissed him off. It was no different that evening, and Mike hung up on his dad. Even though it was hard to hear their conversation, I knew that Allan is usually right on target. I hoped Mike had been thinking and praying about what he had done, what it might mean for him, and what his plan B might be, if needed.

Allan and I prayed together for Mike before we went to bed. It felt good to do that, like we were a team rooting for the underdog. Whatever happened, we wanted God's will for Mike. We believed God's plan was superior to any plan we could imagine. I woke up throughout the night and prayed for Mikey again. Surprisingly, I didn't feel stressed or anxious about the situation. Once we found out what would happen, we'd go from there.

I received several encouraging emails from our friends who were praying. I felt so loved and cared for by our friends and their prayers and words of encouragement. All I could do was wait for the outcome, whatever that might be.

As I was waiting to hear back from Hazelden, I recalled

how I looked forward to my calls from Mike. I missed him so much. He was my talker and the son who spent the most time with me. I missed that connection. I went through my days like normal, but really, there's no longer a normal when dealing with addiction. I felt alone a lot of the time. My friends were there, but they didn't understand what was going on. I talked to God a lot. He was working in me as much as He was in Mike.

On Wednesday I stayed home all day, waiting to hear from Mike or his counselor. I tried to stay busy with cleaning, doing laundry, checking emails, and praying. Mike called late in the afternoon. He said he had met for three hours with Noelle, another counselor named Amy, and one other unnamed person. Mike didn't elaborate on their conversation, but he said they were giving him a choice to stay in treatment and work—really work—on his addiction or to discharge himself.

Suddenly Mike yelled over the receiver, "I want to leave. I hate it here!"

Taken aback, I replied, "Mike, that's a bad idea. You need to be there and continue to get help for your addiction."

"Mom, if I come home, I will go to AA meetings. I will get a sponsor. I will work on the steps."

"No, Mike, you need to stay there! You don't have enough skills or tools to make it on your own."

"But you don't know that, Mom! I think I can do it on my own. I want to at least try."

"Listen, Mike, I know you want to come home. You miss your family. But I'm worried that when the first bump in the road comes along, or you have a bad relationship, you will use again."

"Mom, I promise you: I won't use. Please just let me come home."

The conversation continued for another twenty minutes, him going on and on about leaving and me telling him he needed to stay. Mike was adamant that he wanted to leave. The discussion was intense. I could feel the energy draining out of me as we cycled again through the arguments.

There's a saying that insanity is doing the same things over and over and expecting different results. Thinking back to that conversation, that's exactly how I felt. I believe he was still in the height of his addiction.

At the end of the call, I told him to think long and hard about leaving and asked him to call us before doing anything.

I tried to rephrase my concerns: "Mike, you're an addict. You need more time beyond the two weeks you've been there, and you need the continued help to beat this addiction."

After we hung up, I called Noelle and left a voice message. When I didn't hear back from her, I called Amy and left a message with her. I was at my wits' end.

Noelle called me back later in the evening and apologized for not calling sooner. Allan got on the line to listen in as she talked about the events of the past couple days and Mike's call to me.

While we talked, our call waiting beeped and I saw that it was Mike. We ended our conversation with Noelle, and I talked with Mike. He told me he'd decided to stay. He agreed with what I had told him earlier. He said he knew that the decision to leave treatment could literally kill him. The conversation was curt and short.

Extremely relieved, I called Noelle back to let her know. She was glad to hear of his decision. She said Mike needed to walk the walk, not just talk the talk. We agreed to wait and see how the next few days would go. She stated that Mike needed to go forward and make some choices while he continued there.

Before we hung up, I asked her about restrictions that Allan and I might need to have in place if Mike left. I had done some research on substance abuse and relapse, and I knew he would need rules to help him move forward in recovery without the daily structure of the center. We discussed the following restrictions: Mike could not live at our home; he would have to find employment to cover living expenses; he could not have his car, cell phone, or wallet; and, Noelle added, he would need to attend outpatient rehab and treatment. Outpatient is less restrictive than inpatient. It usually requires ten to twelve hours a week at a local treatment center while allowing the recovering user to keep going to work or school.[8] Mike would also need to attend AA or Narcotics Anonymous (NA) meetings. Noelle said each of those restrictions was perfectly appropriate, and she emphasized that Allan and I would need to follow through on them. Mike needed to understand how serious we were about having the restrictions in place before he decided to leave. From my research I knew that consistency and enforcement of restrictions would be important for all of us. Mike would need to know that his counselor, Allan, and I were all on the same page.

Mike called on Thursday afternoon. He seemed much more upbeat. His group had gone to a day camp that morning to work on building trust among team members. I knew he loved outdoor activities like bungee jumping and rappelling down walls, so this was right up his alley. It seemed like a good way for him to build some trust in others.

He didn't talk long to me. He asked if Sean was around. He told me he missed his brother, who he'd been avoiding since arriving at Hazelden. I think Mike felt ashamed about lying to Sean about his drug use and thought that the trust they had shared had been severed. To me, it was a good sign that Mike was beginning to understand how his disease had hurt Sean and was willing to reach out and try to repair their relationship.

Sean was home and eager to talk to his brother. Soon I heard Sean laughing and joking with Mike. It did my soul good to hear that. It seemed like old times. Afterward I could tell that Sean was really glad to have talked to his brother. It would take some time for Sean and Mike to restore their relationship, but this was a good start.

5. The Family Program

During Mike's treatment, Allan and I took advantage of a four-day family program offered by Hazelden. One family member could attend for free, and others had to pay a fee. It doesn't seem expensive in retrospect, given the wealth of knowledge we received. We attended the session from Sunday, August 17, to Wednesday, August 20, 2008.

We learned so much about substance use disorder: its causes, the effects of drugs and alcohol on the brain, and the different classes of drugs. We began to understand Mike's drug of choice. We listened to lectures by counselors, watched informative DVDs, and did role-play with the other family members. Each day's information built on the previous days' learning. The program was extremely enlightening, and, in the days to come, we would rely heavily on what we'd learned.

Ultimately, we came to understand that this was Mike's problem and he needed to learn how to manage it. We identified what was our responsibility and what was his. We were introduced to terms like *enabling* and *rescuing* our loved ones. We learned about recovery: his and our own.

I came away with one outstanding insight: I was just as

"addicted" to Mike as he was to heroin. There are similar patterns in how those who misuse substances and loved ones of those who use become obsessed with their drug of choice.

Beverly Conyers, in an article titled "Are You Addicted to Your Addicted Child?," writes, "For a long time after discovering that my daughter was addicted to heroin, I was so obsessed with trying to fix her that I had no life of my own. She became my sole source of comfort (when I could convince myself that she was getting better) and my deepest source of pain (when her struggles were too obvious to ignore). It was almost as if her addiction controlled us both." Conyers lists sixteen behaviors that indicate you are possibly addicted to your child, and I exhibited several. I constantly thought about Mike: what he was doing, where he was, how he was. I'd find myself searching through his drawers, looking for evidence of drugs. I'd pump his friends for information on his whereabouts and activities and check up on him by calling him "to see how his day was," listening for every inflection in his tone of voice to see if he was high or lying to me. I neglected my family and friends in order to always be available for Mikey. Later, when Mike was in Colorado, he would call me to ask if I would deposit money in his account. I'd jump in my car and drive to my bank to make a cash withdrawal, then head to Mike's bank and deposit the cash into his account. Why cash? Cash deposits can immediately be withdrawn. Then I'd call Mike to tell him the money was deposited. He claimed he needed it to pay rent or his cell-phone bill or buy groceries, but in reality, he was buying drugs. Did I know that? Yes, I did!

But I did it anyway because, in my mind, I was "helping" my son—the insanity of both of our addictions.

Conyers continues, "But when these types of behaviors become a consistent pattern—when they diminish our ability to live our own life—it's possible they've become an addiction. The good news is that by living *our own life* to the best of our ability, we're better able to offer the clarity and consistency that can be of genuine help to our addicted child."[9]

During the family program, I came to truly understand how Mike's illness was changing my life. It was a harsh discovery to find that I was behaving like an addict. We learned about the daily battle of staying clean and sober and that you're always only one step away from relapse. Each day was extremely intense, and we came home exhausted.

We came to understand it is a family disease because everyone in the family is affected by it. As an example, we spent Dan's birthday in the program and had to postpone celebrating with him. Dan said he understood, but this was only one of many family celebrations that were interrupted or never celebrated during Mike's four-year battle with addiction. I know this angered Dan and Sean. To them it seemed the world revolved around Mike and his disease, whether he was actively using or in recovery. They were truly justified in their thinking, but they were gracious enough not to take their anger or frustration out on Mike or me.

A few months later I would have a wrenching example of the disease's effects. I was talking to Sean in the kitchen when Mike came in through the back door. I immediately stopped talking with Sean and began conversing with Mike. I don't remember what seemed so important. Sean and I never finished our conversation. I remember Sean looking at us and then sadly walking away. Later that day, after Mike had left, I apologized to Sean for leaving our talk. Sean said something I will never forget: "That's okay, Mom, that always happens when Mike comes home."

It felt like I had been stabbed in the heart. That was one of the first times I realized just how much Mike's substance use was affecting our family.

The family program was also the first time that Allan and I felt we were not alone on this journey. Other parents were going through the same ordeals with their children, and we received and returned support and understanding from other parents, which is paramount. We were emotionally bound together during those days. Their story was our story, their fears our fears; the characters were different in each story, as was the drug of choice, but they were struggling just as we were struggling. We laughed, we cried, we hugged as we shared the intimate details of living with a person who has a substance use disorder. And, for the first time since I learned of Mikey's disease, I felt hope.

We saw Mike during the family program. It was usually just a short visit at lunch, but I relished those few minutes each day with him.

At lunch on Monday, Mike told us he was thinking about discharging himself. He didn't like it there and wanted out; we translated that he wanted to get out to use. My anxiety level rose, my heart began to pound, and my hands sweated as Mike talked about wanting to leave. Allan and I had just done some role-playing on this very topic in the morning session. I decided to try out what I had learned.

I looked at Mike directly in his eyes. "I feel very scared that you want to leave here to go out and use drugs, knowing that it could kill you. It will not be my fault if you die, but it will devastate our family forever. You have two brothers who love you, and you will devastate their lives as well," I said as a tear rolled down my cheek.

He looked down at his hands. "I just want to leave and use."

"I want you to stay. But if you choose to leave, you need to seriously consider the consequences of that decision."

He nodded and got up from the table and walked away.

I figured that Noelle would get ahold of us if Mike decided to discharge himself. We left at the end of the day, exhausted.

We arrived the next morning, Tuesday, ready for another long day. At noon we met Mike for lunch.

"I'm going to discharge myself today. I can't be here any longer."

I felt my anxiety rising again. I pushed it down and took a deep breath. Just then Noelle walked into the lunchroom and sat beside Mike.

"How's it going today, Mike?"

"I'm going to discharge myself this afternoon. I can't take being clean any longer!" He gave her a steely look.

She answered, "Why don't we take a walk to my office and discuss this?" We all followed her back into her office, where she said, "So tell me, Mike, what's going on?"

"I can't do recovery any longer. I'm not strong enough." He began to sob. "I don't have any fight left in me."

Allan and I got up from our chairs and held him tightly.

"We love you. We will support you, but if you choose to leave, we will not stop you," I said.

Allan added, "Mike, you've never backed down from a fight before. You are a fighter! You can fight this. But you have to fight for yourself."

Mike wrapped his arms around Allan's neck, sobbing so hard he could barely get his words out. "I . . . can't . . . do . . . this. It's . . . too . . . hard. I don't have the strength to fight this."

"Oh yes you do!" I said. "This isn't you talking, Mike, it's your addiction. You can do this. You're bigger and stronger than this addiction."

Allan took Mike's hands in his and looked him in the eyes. "You can kick this addiction's ass if you want to. I want you to visually put your addiction on the floor and stomp on it because that's where it belongs. Your addiction is separate from who you are and who you can be."

"I don't understand why you love me; I don't even love myself." He fell back into his dad's arms, sobbing.

"Mom and I will love you until you can love yourself. We have enough love for both. We will stand alongside you and hold you up. But you have to do the hard work of recovery."

"We will be here for you. So will your counselor, the staff, and your peers. You are not alone in this battle, Mike!" I firmly stated.

This episode lasted nearly forty minutes. We were all completely drained, but Allan needed to go to work for a couple of hours, and I needed to go back to the afternoon session. We left Mike with his counselor to process what had just happened. Later, Mike joined me in the family program just in time to watch a DVD on relapse.

After the DVD was over, I asked Mike if he'd made a decision. He told me he knew he needed to stay there even though he wanted to leave. After the last session of the day, Allan returned and the three of us went back to Noelle's office for some closure. Over time, we would recognize that afternoon as a defining moment for Mike.

Mike stated repeatedly, "God was there in that room, and God has been with me all this time. I should have been dead several times over, but I'm not. It was like a veil had been lifted. I had clarity, I was able to think clearly, and my anxiety was completely gone."

Personally, I believe there was a spiritual battle going on for Mike's soul in that office. We were fighting for his very life that day. It was scary and awesome at the same time.

Mike shared with me that Noelle had told him she'd never encountered a situation of that magnitude during her time as a counselor. When Mike broke down and fell into Allan's arms, she actually felt the oppression begin to lift.

Thinking back to that day, it's pretty amazing what God did. God had a plan for Mike that day, one that had spiritual implications. Coincidently, that morning I had emailed out a prayer request to our friends asking for a breakthrough for Mike. I know we had many people praying for Mike that day, and I saw the power of those prayers answered in that room. It had indeed been a breakthrough for him.

Allan and I finished the family program Wednesday afternoon. The parents, siblings, other close family members, and friends who had attended the program gathered together to share what they had learned and what they were going to do for their recovery. Each one received a medallion with the Serenity Prayer imprinted on it (see the back of this book). The staff shared what it was like for them to watch this group learn and grow. It was a very moving and enlightening time.

We ended the program by gathering in a circle, holding hands, and saying the Serenity Prayer. I had learned so much in those four days. I felt stronger and more confident in myself. Little did I know how much I would come to rely on the information I'd gained. Finally, we received what we had waited for all week: a three-hour pass with our child.

We picked up Mike and headed to the local mall. I was ecstatic. We had dinner, did some shopping for Mike, and just hung out. We ran into other families from the program at the mall too. We ended up at a local park to play catch with Mike. The three of us cherished this time together, but before we knew it, our three hours were up and it was time to take him back. As we said our goodbyes to Mike, I didn't feel as sad as I'd thought I would because he was in the best treatment center in the country. He was getting the help he needed, and I could see he was starting to understand the hold this addiction had over him. I was hopeful that this treatment would be the only one he'd need.

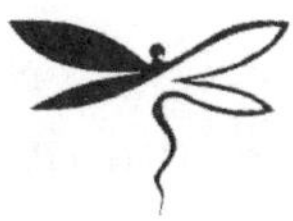

6. Changes Only Mike Can Make

Part of the family program was a family meeting with Mike and one of the counselors. The agenda was Mike's disclosure of his drug history, our response to it, what the treatment program had done for him, and the treatment team's aftercare recommendations. I was a little on edge when we started because I had no idea what he was about to reveal to us. He began,

> I started using marijuana when I was thirteen or fourteen. I used mostly at parties with my friends. In ninth or tenth grade I began using opioid-based pills: Percocet, oxycodone, Vicodin. My first introduction to pain pills was from the dentist after having my wisdom teeth pulled. Around age fifteen or sixteen I began dealing drugs to support my habit. I'd sell ten-dollar bags of marijuana and street pills. Street pills are different than prescription pills, more potent and dangerous. One time I had a handgun shoved into my mouth by a drug supplier when I was buying a ten-dollar bag of marijuana. I was terrified I might die but not enough to stop dealing and feeding my habit. When I was working in the summers as a member of a tear-out crew for a carpet company, I would steal pain medications from customers' homes. I'd pretend I needed to use the bathroom, and I would go through the medicine cabinets

> looking for prescription medications. When I found medications, I would pilfer the pills but not enough to raise suspicion.
>
> I stole and sold items that were stored in our attic in order to purchase drugs: TVs, lamps, MP3 players, CDs, or anything I could take that you wouldn't notice missing. I sold gifts you had bought: a couple GUESS watches, an iPod, digital cameras, etc. I would tell you I couldn't find them or I'd lost them at a friend's house or they were stolen at school. I took money from your wallets too.

A light went on inside my head as I remembered money going missing from my wallet. It wasn't large amounts of cash, perhaps a ten- or twenty-dollar bill. I didn't carry more than twenty or thirty dollars in my wallet. I'd go to the store to purchase something, and when I went to pay for it my wallet would be empty. I would rack my brain, trying to remember where I'd spent the money I knew I'd had. I'd think I had just forgotten where I spent it. Occasionally Allan would ask me if I'd taken any money out of his wallet. I'd say no, and he'd say, "I could swear I had a ten or twenty in there last night." Again, we'd assume he'd spent it, not even considering one of our children would steal from us.

Mike continued his story:

> The first time I used heroin was Memorial Day weekend 2008, a few weeks before the BWCA weekend. Nick and I drove to Colorado to visit Flynn. The three of us had played hockey during our elementary and junior high years. Nick and Flynn had been using OxyContin for

> some time before that, snorting it. Flynn got hooked on it after he broke his arm and had surgery. They used it recreationally with friends. I think their abuse of drugs had got pretty bad, and I believe that's when Nick decided to move back to Minnesota. At the time when Nick and I made the trip to Colorado, OxyContin was becoming harder to find, also much more expensive, and that's when black tar [a form of heroin] became popular in our circle of friends. We would dilute the tar in warm water inside of Visine bottles and sniff that, but it didn't take long after that to get into needles.
>
> That first high was the most amazing feeling I've ever experienced. I had the sensation of complete well-being. I felt such happiness. I was so relaxed, my body going jelly-like. I was always chasing that first high again and again. But it always eluded me.

My heart ached as he told us his story. It was hard to believe that our son had done these things to support his habit. I tried to remain objective and not allow my expression to change, but it was very difficult to hear what he was telling us. I felt sad, angry, and disappointed. But then a new sensation bubbled up inside me: pity. For him and where his illness had taken him.

Next, I gave Mike my feedback: "Mike, I felt so scared when I heard about the gun shoved into your mouth and how terrified you must have been. I'm so very disappointed that you stole from us. I felt violated multiple times as you spoke. And it is unfathomable to me that you could have total disregard for values we'd instilled in you. And as sad and scared as I feel learning about your drug use, I still love you very much. Nothing will ever change that. I hope you know that."

Then Noelle shared her recommendations for Mike's aftercare, starting with the ninety-day extended-care program housed at the Plymouth location. Everyone agreed it was the best place for Mike to go. He still needed a lot of support; he needed more skills and tools to stay clean and sober when he was on his own. The meeting ended on a positive and upbeat note, especially for Mike. "A treatment high," his counselor said.

Mike was scheduled for release from the program late in August 2008. He was accepted into the extended-care program, but unfortunately the choices he made in his last couple of weeks there—such as not finishing his assignments, huffing and lying about it, and fraternizing with the female patients—as well as his ambivalence about finishing the program gave the staff second thoughts. It is important for the addict to fully engage in his part of the recovery program. The infractions he committed may seem minor, but they showed his inability to understand the importance of following the rules in treatment and eventually in returning to life on his own. In the end, he was unable to enter the ninety-day program. Allan and I were very disappointed.

I knew enough about Mike's illness by then to know he needed more help. He had made a good start on understanding his disease and what steps he needed to work on, but he had not made a lot of progress. He was still struggling with getting his anxiety under control, knowing that it was a trigger for using. Each day is a battle for the person with substance use disorder, and I felt he hadn't developed the tools to stay clean and sober. So much of recovery relies on the skills learned in treatment, and I was concerned he would relapse at the first bump he encountered. Since he was not in the extended-care program, we did not allow Mike to live with us or have his car until he completed further steps toward recovery. That may sound harsh, but it was the right thing to do. We needed to help Mike break the chain of using.

Throughout this entire ordeal, Mike knew one thing: his family loved him unconditionally and would be there for him no matter what. Mike was unable to love himself or believe in himself when it came to beating his illness. We loved Mike more than he loved himself. We knew he needed to make some changes in his life, and we put pressure on him to make them—changes only Mike could make.

Mike was discharged from Hazelden on August 26, and he took a cab to our house. We'd told Mike he could be at our house as long as someone was home, but he wasn't allowed to sleep there, per the restrictions we had all agreed upon.

When he arrived at the house, he dropped his suitcases in the living room and started walking around. He went into each room. He opened cabinet doors, he looked in the closets, and he sat on his bed and bounced on it. I sensed he was savoring his time back home—just really happy to be there. I think he took a nap too. Later that afternoon he went to the garage to get his bike. He said he was going to get something to eat and wouldn't be gone for long. He was gone for several hours. When he returned, he told me he'd hooked up with an old friend from school and would stay with him that first night.

Before leaving for his friend's house, Mike told Allan and me that he'd come up with a plan. He seemed excited about it, and we hoped this plan would help him stay on the path of recovery. Mike's plan was

1. Attend AA meetings five times a week

2. Get a sponsor (someone who is further along in their recovery and willing to spend time helping you work on the steps of recovery)

3. Enroll in a Twelve-Step outpatient treatment program

4. Secure a part-time job

5. Random drug testing

6. 1:00 a.m. curfew

And, of course, no drug use.

Allan and I told Mike we wanted everything written in the form of a contract that the three of us would sign. He reluctantly agreed to do it and typed the contract on the computer. We read it over together, but no one signed it. I'm not sure why we didn't. Mike was antsy to leave, and Allan and I were still struggling with the events of the past month and didn't have the emotional strength to demand it, so we let it go for the time being. We explained to Mike that after he complied with the terms of the contract, we would revisit having him move home.

That night Allan went with Mike to his first AA meeting.

The steps and principles used in this peer-delivered mutual self-help model are helpful for anyone who struggles with any form of addictive behavior, and branches include NA, Marijuana Anonymous, and Overeaters Anonymous. At an AA meeting, selected speakers share their experience of how their lives changed when they joined AA and what practices aid them in staying away from the problem substance, according to the speaker's experiences. In some sessions, meeting providers share the Twelve-Step strategy to help those with substance use disorder to stay away from their drug of choice. This model is used at Hazelden Betty Ford, where Mike first encountered it, and many other treatment centers.

Allan said Mike was as nervous as a six-year-old boy on his first day of kindergarten. Because AA meetings are designed for the person with substance use disorder, Allan had to wait outside for Mike. (Family members and friends of chemically dependent people can attend Al-Anon.) The meeting was good for Mike. He told Allan the meetings kept him out of his head and grounded him in sober living. He met other recovering people, including Eli, who agreed to be Mike's temporary sponsor.

The poem that follows is written from the addictive substance's perspective and circulates anonymously through many recovery websites. I find it to be a very honest and eye-opening piece. Drug addiction is no respecter of persons. It doesn't discriminate based on race, gender, or sexual orientation. Whether you have a PhD or a GED, you're fair game. It doesn't care about how financially well off you are. Eventually it will acquire all your resources. All addiction cares about is getting its talons into you and never letting go.

Hello, My Name is DRUGS

I destroy homes. I tear families apart—
take your children, and that's just the start.
I'm more costly than diamonds, more costly than gold;
the sorrow I bring is a sight to behold.
If you need me, remember: I'm easily found.
I live all around you, in schools and in town.
I live with the rich. I live with the poor.
I live down the street and maybe next door.
My power is awesome—try me, you'll see.
But if you do, you may never break free.
Just try me once, and I might let you go,
but try me twice, then I own your soul.
When I possess you, you'll steal and you'll lie.
You'll do what you have to just to get high.
The crimes you'll commit for my narcotic charms,
will be worth the pleasure you'll feel in your arms.
You'll lie to your mother. You'll steal from your dad.
When you see their tears, you should feel sad.
But you'll forget your morals and how you were raised.
I'll be your conscience; I'll teach you my ways.
I take kids from their parents. I take parents from kids.
I turn people from God. I separate friends.
I'll take everything from you, your looks, and your pride;
I'll be with you always, right by your side.
You'll give up everything—your family, your home,
your money, your friends, then you'll be alone.
I'll take and I'll take, till you've no more to give.
When I finish with you, you'll be lucky to live.

If you try me be warned this is no game.
If I'm given the chance, I'll drive you insane.
I'll ravage your body. I'll control your mind.
I'll own you completely; your soul will be mine.
The nightmares I'll give you when you're lying in bed;
and the voices you'll hear from inside your head;
The sweats, the shakes, and the visions you'll see,
I want you to know, these are all gifts from me.
But then it's too late, and you'll know in your heart,
that you are mine and we shall not part.
You'll regret that you tried me, they always do.
But you came to me, not me to you.
You knew this would happen.
Many times you were told,
but you challenged my power, and you chose to be bold.
You could have said no and just walked away.
If you could live that day over, now what would you say?
I'll be your master; you'll be my slave.
I'll even go with you when you go to your grave.
Now that you've met me, what will you do?
Will you try me or not?
It's all up to you.
I can bring you more misery than words can tell.
Come, take my hand, and let me lead you to Hell.

Signed,

DRUGS

7. Mike's First Relapse

On Friday morning, August 29, I flew to South Carolina with my sister Candee to attend the funeral of our aunt Sharon, who had passed away after a long battle with breast cancer. Allan picked me up at the airport on Tuesday, and on the way home he described his weekend with Mike.

> On his second or third evening after being discharged from the program, Mike told me he ran into a guy from the treatment center at an AA meeting and was going to stay with him. He packed a bag and left. I didn't see him until a few nights later when he showed up at the house to get some more clothes and sign the contract—or so I thought.
>
> I was enjoying a pleasant summer evening on our back deck when Mike dropped the bombshell: he had started using heroin the day he was discharged.
>
> My pleasant evening was suddenly hijacked. I tried to process this revelation. I was thrust back in time to those conversations we had with Mike when he wanted to leave Hazelden and use. Nothing can prepare you for such disastrous news.

He said, "I'm sorry, Dad. I just had to use. I didn't want to come back here that night to have you see me high. I wish I could stop this, but I can't."

I told him, "Oh, Mike, NO! You didn't use again! You just got out of treatment."

His eyes avoided mine as he said, "I feel so ashamed. I hope you can try to understand."

Then Mike walked into the house. I heard him on the phone. Mike called Eli to tell him about the relapse. It wasn't long before Eli and a friend of his, Mark, showed up at our house. Eli told Mike to flush the remaining heroin down the toilet, which he did. Eli told us he was going to help Mike look for a sober house to live in. They helped Mikey pack some things in a duffel bag. Mark told me that Mike could stay with him until he found a sober house to live in.

I spent thirty minutes that evening talking with Eli and Mark about substance use disorder and recovery. They talked about how AA had been their saving grace, a place they found with people who genuinely cared for them despite their disease.

Then, with duffel bag in hand, the three of them left our house to go to an AA meeting. Later I thought to myself, *I must be going nuts—here I am handing my newly sober son over to two perfect strangers, recovering people no less, his life and well-being in their hands.* But I was very much at peace with that.

Friday evening the doorbell rang. It was one of those moments where you know things are not good. There at the door stood Eli with bad news. Mike had used again and had called Mark, saying he wanted to end his life.

Mike wouldn't say where he was except that he was at a park near our home. I knew of no park nearby, but Eli indicated we needed to find him soon. I said a prayer before leaving with Eli, me in my car and him on his motorcycle. Two blocks from the house I looked down the street toward the neighborhood school and saw Mike. We raced over to Mike; he didn't run. At the same time, two other cars showed up with friends from AA that Mike had called.

Eli told me I needed to get Mike to detox immediately. I called 911. The dispatcher told me to take him to Riverside Detox and Treatment Center in Minneapolis. I drove Mike there, and within two hours he was released. As it turned out, he hadn't used long enough or ingested enough heroin to qualify for detox. Mike would have to detox at home. We returned to the house.

I brought Mike home with the understanding he would not leave the house alone until you returned from South Carolina, and we could get him into another residential treatment program. Mike agreed to the terms. He told me he knew he needed more help with his disease. Mike couldn't leave the yard, and I would be with him at all times. Basically, he was under house arrest. We were joined at the hip the rest of the weekend. I took his wallet but let him keep his cell phone.

The first twenty-four hours went well, but on Saturday

afternoon Dan came over after work to give me a break so I could go for a bike ride and run a few errands. Before I left, Mike asked for his cash card back so he could pay his cell-phone bill. I reluctantly gave the card to him. When I returned from my bike ride and errands, I asked Mike for the cash card back and he told me, "I must have lost it, I don't have it." Oh, I was so frustrated at that point! I had Mike call the bank to cancel the card. The teller told us Mike's last withdrawal had been for eighty dollars less than an hour ago.

Right away, Dan and I grilled Mike about that transaction. Finally, Mike admitted he'd left his cash card on the front porch and someone picked it up to buy heroin for him. The dilemma now was to find where the drugs had been dropped off. Mike refused to give us that information. Then Mike tried to leave the house, saying he was going to a friend's, but we knew that he was going to use. Mike tried to bolt out of the front door, but Dan grabbed him and held his arms around him to keep him there. After a short struggle Mike broke down crying. He told Dan the heroin was inside a balloon by the side of our garage. Dan retrieved the drugs and flushed them down the toilet.

A word on relapse: the National Institute on Drug Abuse states that more than 85 percent of people with addictions who stop using a drug begin using it again within a year.[10] If a recovering person's skills are not yet strong enough, they may relapse even when they know that there will be physical, social, and even legal consequences.

I was beginning to think the twenty-eight days of Mike's treatment had been a waste of time and money, not to mention the emotional toll it was taking on our family. This situation felt overwhelming. Allan continued,

> Sunday, Mike wanted to get out of the house and go for a ride. I drove him to a local AA meeting, but he refused to go in. Instead we ended up at the Mississippi River and sat on the rocks while we talked. I drove Mike back to the house, and we spent the rest of the day inside. Mike was ornery and out of sorts: detox was clearly having an impact.
>
> Sean had been gone for the weekend. When he got home, I told him what was going on. I asked Sean to stay at the house so I could get out for a little while. Later in the afternoon Dan came by, and the four of us barbecued steaks for dinner. Mike seemed to have settled down a bit. Dan left after dinner around 9:00 p.m. Then Mike started threatening to leave the house. You know what Mike was thinking, right? Mike had it all figured out—he would use again until he was admitted for treatment where he could undergo detox with drugs to help him withdraw. Sean and I managed to keep Mike home, though I believe the main reason was he had no resources to purchase drugs.
>
> Today when I went to work, I've never been so grateful in my life to be there. Sean agreed to stay home with Mike until I could pick you up. Midmorning, Sean called me, panicked. Mike had run out of the house and jumped into a "friend's" car—no friend at all but a fellow user.
>
> I told Sean that it wasn't his fault. If Dan or I had been home, Mike would have done the same thing. Both of them called Mike, but he wouldn't answer his phone. A short time later I received two text messages from Mike.

> The first one stated, *I'm okay but couldn't sit at the house anymore. I had to use because I was going crazy. I don't want to talk to you, but I'm okay.* The second text was, *I didn't shoot up. I'll be back to the house in twenty minutes to sit on the front porch.* Mike called me on the way back to the house to apologize for what he'd put Sean and me through. Mike admitted to me that he is truly powerless over his heroin use and needs inpatient treatment.

I was truly sad to hear about Allan's weekend with Mike. I felt a little guilty for not being there, even though going to the funeral was the right thing to do. I was able to be with family as we grieved for my aunt, but it also gave me some physical distance and respite from what was happening at home. Mike and I would have to find another treatment center as soon as possible, but that task could wait until tomorrow. I was exhausted.

Later that evening, three of Mike's non-using friends showed up at the house and spent an hour talking with him. Mike said he enjoyed having his friends over. I was grateful for the support they showed—it was what Mike needed right now. In his eulogy for Mike, Allan recalled how important those friends had been, saying, "Mike was born in Saint Paul and spent his entire life here in the same neighborhood until two years ago. That gave Mike a true gift: a sense of security of growing up with friends that were friends for life. And with two older brothers to watch out for him, as did their friends, life was good for Mike."

Wednesday morning, I called Blue Cross Blue Shield and explained I was looking for long-term treatment center options for Mike that were covered under his plan. I made call after call to treatment centers all over Minnesota, but none had any immediate openings. I didn't think we could manage two weeks with Mike at home in his current condition. I was beginning to feel hopeless.

My last call was to Project Turnabout (P-Tab), a non-profit inpatient center two hours west of the Twin Cities. Its ninety-day program came highly recommended, but, unfortunately, they too had no openings for at least two weeks. That was the last straw. Frustrated, I threw the phone number at Mike and yelled "You need to find a place yourself! I can't do this for you!" as I stalked out the door to my retreat in the backyard.

Several minutes later, Mike burst out the back door, excitement in his voice as he said, "Mom, I can get into Project Turnabout tomorrow. They will have an opening for me!"

I was stunned but very grateful. Mike needed to do his own work to get into a center, but I had taken over that job. When I handed it back to him, he took responsibility for his disease. He told me a counselor had done an intake assessment over the phone and admitted him into the program. Mike now needed to download the information he'd need from their website, including what to bring, what to leave at home, and what rules and regulations he'd need to follow at the center.

He was so excited; he seemed ready to battle his disease again. Mike called his dad and told him the good news. Allan and I were ecstatic. Mike was going to get the help he needed, and we hoped we could resume our normal lives.

That evening the five of us ate dinner on our back deck. We barbecued hamburgers and made oven-baked fries, and the boys drank a few beers as we spent time as a family. It seemed like old times as we laughed and joked during dinner and the guys played catch out front. Everyone was in high spirits, especially Mike. Still, I had a hard time sleeping that night in anticipation of Mike entering his second treatment center since our family intervention less than six weeks ago.

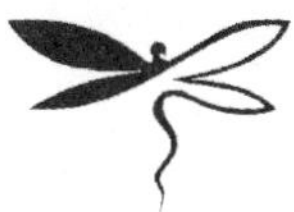

8. Powerlessness

It felt like we were on a roller coaster—you know the kind I'm talking about, where you are strapped into a metal car on elevated tracks. When Mike went into treatment, we knew it would be a rough ride. But when you hear the click of the bar locking into place in your car, you feel safe, just as I felt secure having a plan for Mike's illness. With a lurch, the coaster car slowly pulls away from the safety of the platform. I could feel my nice, normal life retreating behind me. Looming in front of you is the steep climb of the unknown. Up, up, up you go, climbing higher and higher. You can see the entire park below you for a few moments. I had my entire life planned out. The view looked spectacular back then. You look up just as you crest the hill—and go flying down the other side into corkscrew inversions and tight corners, climbing steep slopes and plummeting again, jerking this way and that at what feel like astonishing speeds, screaming at the top of your lungs. You feel like you've been turned inside out.

I held on for dear life during Mike's first round in treatment, hoping and praying I wouldn't fly out of my seat to my death, rising out of my seat and slamming back down as I flew around the track. Normally the ride suddenly ends, with your throat raw from screaming and your heart pounding as you wait for the attendant to release you. Others exit, rushing off with smiles and laughter to try something else, or even get back in line, and finally the attendant unlocks your car. But I couldn't leave this ride. Before I could catch my breath, it took off again, speeding up and down, around and over. Over the next months we wondered every day when or if we could get off as Mike used, pursued sobriety, and relapsed time after time.

On Thursday morning, I woke Mike up as I was heading to the shower and told him to be ready in thirty minutes, as we needed to be at P-Tab in Granite Falls before noon. After my shower I could see that Mike had gotten up; I assumed he was in the basement, showering, and had packed his things in the car. I headed downstairs to the kitchen and, as I rounded the corner, noticed a sheet of paper lying on the floor at the bottom of the stairs. I picked it up and read it.

Mom, I had to use one more time! I'll be back soon. I love you, and don't worry.

Fear's talons gripped my heart and squeezed the breath out of me as Mike's note fluttered to the floor. I fell to my knees and cried out, "Oh, God, no, not now, not when we're so close!"

As I lay on my kitchen floor, sobbing, I pleaded with God to keep Mike safe, bring him home, and not let him get any bad shit. It felt like I was there for hours, sobbing, praying, and pleading. I could barely catch my breath between sobs.

Then fear hissed in my ear, "He's not coming back; he's going to die." The voice was so loud it drowned out my own pounding heart.

Then a thought—no, more an enlightenment—dawned on me: *So this is what powerlessness feels like. I am powerless over Mike's choices, whether he chooses to use or decides to get help.* And at that moment I felt powerless over my own life. I realized that I was experiencing the first step of AA: "We admitted we were powerless over alcohol [and drugs and other people's addiction]—that our lives had become unmanageable." Well, hell, if this scene in my kitchen wasn't unmanageability, then I didn't know what was.

With this understanding, fear's talons loosened their grip on my heart, on me. "I truly have no power over this," I said out loud for the first time. Then, ever so slowly, I came to my knees. The note lying on the floor in front of me no longer held its power.

I knew I had no control over what might come next. I had to reach out to something or someone. I recalled the second step, "Came to believe that a power greater than ourselves could restore us to sanity." *I must be living a life of insanity,* I told myself. *Yep, that's what it feels like.* I was able to stand up. I was not steady on my feet, but I was upright. I grabbed the note and shredded it with everything I had in me.

My breathing slowed to normal. I began to pray with a strength and power I hadn't had just moments earlier. *I can do this. I must do this,* I told myself, and I felt hope wash over me. Suddenly the room felt lighter and brighter, as if the sunshine had somehow filtered into my heart and soul.

Just then Mike strolled into the house, smiling. I knew he was high, but that didn't alter my current state of mind.

"I'll be ready to go in twenty minutes," he said.

He said it like he had just gone out to pick up a loaf of

bread or a pack of cigarettes instead of his drug of choice. He was completely unaware that I had just gone through an internal struggle against one of my greatest fears and begun my own journey through the Twelve Steps of AA.

I took a deep breath. I chose to let go of my fear. I released Mike to God and asked Him to intervene, knowing that, somehow, He would. And I knew He would get me through this day and those to come. Fear was no longer my traveling companion. That day I let go—not perfectly, but it was a start. It was also the beginning of the next step, "Made a decision to turn our will and lives over to the care of God as we understood Him."

I made it through that day and the next ones that came along, as they say in AA, one day at a time.

I have not forgotten the lesson of just how powerless I was that day. I am powerless over many things in my life, but I cannot allow fear to control me. Occasionally I forget and the lesson comes back to me. Then, once again, I turn my will and life over to the care of God to allow Him control over the situation that I am so powerless to change.

9. The Gift of Love and Support

Mike was in a jovial mood as we made our way to Granite Falls. He chatted with me between phone calls to his friends, telling them about his heroin addiction and that he was on his way to treatment. He wrote down their phone numbers and addresses and promised to call and write them. We stopped several times on the way there for food, gas, and bathroom breaks. Mike and I talked about what his next three months might be like. I told him we'd visit as often as we could. He spoke about how he hated his addiction and was so ready to be at P-Tab.

We arrived on the campus a little before noon. It was a warm and sunny day. Mike unloaded his bags and left them at the front desk to be searched for contraband. We proceeded to the intake office. We sat together as the counselor asked Mike about his drug history. Partway through Mike said he felt sick, like he was going to throw up. She asked Mike if he'd been using on the way there. He said he had been.

My mouth fell open; I couldn't believe it. I hadn't seen him using. He must have seen my stunned expression.

"Mom, I'm sorry. I didn't want you to know. I knew you'd

be upset with me. But that's what addicts do: use one last time before treatment." He wouldn't look at me after that.

Now I felt like the one who was going to be sick. I'd had no idea he was using. In fact, throughout this journey with Mike, Allan and I could not tell when Mike was using or when he was high. Looking back, I can see signs that I missed. When Mike didn't receive his credits in ninth grade, I'd suspected the possibility of drug use. I even went as far as searching his room, but I found no evidence. When I confronted him, he could logically explain away his missing assignments and failed or skipped exams. In tenth grade, Mike sought help for his anxiety from his pediatrician, who prescribed him Xanax. A couple of months after Mike had his three-month prescription filled, he asked me if I had seen his pills. I hadn't. He and I spent an afternoon looking for them. We never found them, and he told me he probably lost them at school. As his drug use progressed, there were other signs, like the mysterious disappearances of small amounts of cash and items stored in our attic. At the time, Allan and I chalked them up to our forgetfulness. Gifts Mike had been given kept coming up missing: a nice watch, an MP3 player, a camera. But we didn't think about all those lost items until Mike admitted that he'd sold them to buy drugs. How naïve we were—and what a good liar Mike was.

A nurse came and took Mike to the detox unit at P-Tab. She told me they would finish his intake there and monitor him for the next few days as he detoxed from the heroin. So, tearfully, I said goodbye to Mike once more. I could tell he just wanted to go and lie down. I watched them walk away, my son's life again in a stranger's hands.

I finished the paperwork necessary for his admission and took a short tour of the facility. It wasn't as prestigious as Hazelden. It was an older facility and had that lived-in look. Some of the rooms needed a coat of paint, the tile floors needed buffing to remove some of the scuffs, and the common room could have been spruced up a bit. But as I learned more about the program, I realized there was more to this place than I initially thought.

The heart of Project Turnabout is the staff's spirit of commitment to helping each patient reclaim the life they thought they lost. The guiding principle is keeping the doors open and costs down so that professional recovery services can be accessible to all. The staff values relationships with patients/clients, working together to establish a partnership that strengthens success.

It was good enough. And far enough from the Twin Cities that I wasn't worried he'd try to leave.

I can't say I was sad as I left, not like I was when we left Mike for the first time at Hazelden. I felt some anger inside, at him and myself. I felt duped by his nonchalant manner as we drove there. I was still processing the fact that Mike had been using during the trip. At that point I didn't understand addiction or the addictive brain. I was glad for this time alone. I listened to CDs, looked at the fall scenery, and prayed for my son. I knew God would take care of Mikey; I just needed to let go of him—again. I needed to remember just how powerless I had felt earlier and how good it had felt to turn my life and will over to the care of God.

I arrived home exhausted. I told Allan about Mike's note, the drive to Project Turnabout, and my drive home. Allan felt empathy for me and, I think, perhaps a little guilt for not being able to accompany us to Granite Falls.

We didn't hear from Mike until the following Monday, four days after he was admitted. Only thirteen days since he was discharged from Hazelden and already in his second inpatient treatment center. He left a message on the house phone that he'd moved out of detox into his unit. He said he'd try to call again later that evening but P-Tab was strict with outgoing phone calls. I waited anxiously for him to call back, and he did several hours later. He seemed tired, and his depression and anxiety had returned. He would be seeing a physician and psychiatrist who would prescribe and monitor his medications. Before we hung up, I told him how proud of him I was for continuing his battle against heroin and that I loved him very much.

Sundays were visiting day at P-Tab. We drove to Granite Falls every week to see Mike. It was a five-hour round trip, and visiting hours were from one until three o'clock in the afternoon. Usually Allan and I came alone. Dan and Sean came several times, and one week we surprised Mike by bringing Grampa Red, Grandma Betty, and Aunt Tracy. When he came into the room and saw them waiting with us, he was speechless, and his face showed pure joy. We greeted him with big hugs. Another week, his friends Greg, Anthony, and Elli, Mike's former girlfriend, made the trek with us. At every visit, Mike always seemed genuinely happy to see us.

Some of the most memorable times we shared with Mike during this four-year battle were Sunday afternoons at P-Tab. Mike often amazed us with his wisdom, which seemed beyond his twenty years. He was brutally honest about everything. It was as if his drug use had forced him into a world of lies and deception, and now that he was free of the drugs, he was liberated. There was no need to hide anything about himself, his thoughts, and his opinions. Mike would offer insights that were surprisingly candid but also logical and perceptive.

Case in point: when the three of us were talking about some people we knew who were facing issues with drinking, Mike explained what the addictive signs were and suggested some ways to talk to them about their drinking. Here was our son, spending a lot of time on his own drug-use issues and yet also taking time to worry about his family's friends and their problems.

We also had discussions about God. Mike believed in a very kind, merciful, loving God who offered forgiveness for sin—especially the sin of drug use. But despite this belief in a God of grace, he was hard on himself for his addiction. He never fell back on God's grace as an excuse for using drugs. After his experience at P-Tab especially, he held himself accountable for his own actions, not relying on God for forgiveness.

One Sunday in November, I couldn't make visiting hours, so Allan went alone. Here's his account of his visit with Mikey.

> It was an amazing time for me. All the visiting rooms were full, so we found a quiet hallway and lay on the floor next to each other and talked. I was amazed at how he had

grown over the past weeks. He was intellectually sharp, inquisitive, perceptive, funny, honest, and sincere. The haze of drugs was disappearing, and the old Mike was returning. Despite all the challenges Mike was facing, I was amazed at his optimism about life. He was a glass-half-full guy. I am an eternal pessimist—a glass is half-empty in my world.

Mike was laying out for me all the challenges ahead of him: finding a place to live, finding a job, meeting new sober friends, and of course staying free from drug use. My thoughts raced ahead of him, imagining all that could go awry. He proceeded to explain how he was going to meet each of these challenges. There was no hint of future failure, no consideration of defeat; only the possibilities of living with sober people and working hourly on his sobriety. That was a lesson on positive thinking I really needed to learn. The attendant came by to give us a five-minute warning that visitation was almost up. I couldn't believe how quickly our two hours had passed.

When I left, I told Mike I thought he was very wise and I looked forward to the day when he got married; he'd make a great husband. And when he had kids he'd impart his wisdom on them.

We saw the power of prayers answered over and over again. This was due in part to the sheer number of people praying for him: family members, friends, friends of friends, people we didn't know who'd heard about Mike's struggles. Allan and I sent letters and cards to Mike nearly every day, and I encouraged those who were praying to send a card, note, or letter to Mike to let him know they were in his corner. Not a week went by that he didn't receive an enormous amount of correspondence, and, although we did not know it then, Mike saved his mail. That explains why he told me, on more than one occasion, that he never understood why so many people cared for him. His dad and I felt loved and supported by those same people as well.

His uncle Michael, my sister's husband, sent Mike several cards. Uncle Michael was a recovering alcoholic and understood Mike and his addiction the best of anyone in our family. He was a straight shooter, and he and Mike had several long-distance discussions followed up by Michael's encouraging cards and notes about recovery. Here is a portion of one of Uncle Michael's letters to Mike:

> As an addict I have found my greatest battlefield is in my mind. I have always struggled with the concepts of others' opinions and lofty goals others have set for me in life. I must admit there were and remain many demons of times past I must deal with on a daily basis, some from family, some from past acquaintances and situations. I feel the excruciating pain you have and continue to endure moment by moment as the mind rushes from one scenario to another, causing frustration, weariness, and eventually ending being trounced by your addictions. I do not have much to offer in this note other than love, hope, and prayer. The mind is like a computer as it processes the information: pictures, scenes, words, thoughts, views, judgments, beliefs, reflections, and meditations we consign to it. The real key is to reset the mind and begin a new data download, but one must do a complete system erase and add a new operating system. As it is said, "Our own best thoughts got us here." These words used to infuriate me to no end; I used

to think, What arrogance they must have to speak to me this way; now I understand it was time for me to have a complete and total mind reset, holding on to none of the old data and loading a new operating system.

The opportunities for a normal life are coming to an end for you, and you know it, I know it, and our family is coming to the realization of it. God has blessed and kept you in many ways over the years. He has a plan for you if you make the choice to allow Him in so He can show you the truth. Do not forget you have this opportunity that you have been given; make the most of it, break free. . . . Love you, Uncle Michael

Mike and his uncle continued to correspond after Mike's time at P-Tab. Uncle Michael was a safe person for Mikey to talk with, and their conversations over the following months helped Mikey as he worked on his sobriety. At one point, Michael gave Mike a cross necklace that his wife had given him. Mike wore that necklace, and I know he cherished the fact that his uncle gave it to him. After Mike died, I returned the necklace to Michael, who has mentioned to me on several occasions how much Mikey helped him even when he was in the midst of relapse. The two of them had a special bond.

Allan wrote to tell Mike about his week, the activities he was involved in, and how work was going; he even compared his workouts to the ones Mike bragged he did at the center. In letters written after a visit, Allan shared the growth he'd seen in Mike or highlighted the amazing conversations they'd had. He'd tell Mike how proud of him he was, how strong he was for working on his addiction. Each letter ended with how much he loved him.

In the letters I sent, I tried to encourage Mike when I knew he was feeling down or discouraged. I could share with Mike on a level that neither his dad nor brothers could because we both struggled with low self-worth and self-esteem and were concerned how others viewed us. In a small way, I also understood his addiction better because I had struggled with an eating disorder since childhood. I had told Mike about it not long after I found out about his heroin addiction.

Food was my comfort and my friend. I ate when I was happy or sad, angry or hurt, and I ate without understanding why. When I crave chocolate, my drug of choice, my mind tells me one of two things. One, say no to the craving and find something else to occupy my mind; once I do that, the craving lessens and I don't give in to it. Or two, begin to entertain the thought of eating "just one bite." I can rationalize purchasing a bar or bag of candy or a pint of my favorite chocolate ice cream by telling myself I'll only eat one serving; I'll feel better, and it'll make me feel happy. The more I think about the chocolate, the more I want it—by that point, if I am honest with myself (which I usually am not), I have already made the decision to head to the store. I continue to rationalize, *Well, I need to pick up a couple things anyway,* which of course is not true. I drive to the store and buy my drug of choice. I come home and unpack the items. I look at the chocolate for just a second: *Only one bite,* I say to myself before I tear open the package. I take that first bite. Yummy! My taste buds wake up. Then those neuropathways in my brain light up, just like what happens to Mike. Before I know it the bar, bag, or pint is gone. The happiness is gone almost as soon as I lay my spoon down. Soon I am awash in guilt and shame, and I vow never to do it again. *Tomorrow,* I think, *I will start fresh....*

It is a vicious cycle and one I have repeated over and over in my life. Still, it has helped me to understand the addict's thought process. "Just one," whether it's the drink, the hit, or the bite, is the end result. It's the process leading up to the use that really begins the relapse.

I experienced deep depression after Mike's relapse. Things went south so fast that I didn't really get a chance to grieve for myself, for the loss of having him around, spending time with him, and seeing him do the things he wanted to do. My disorder erupted as I fell into depression. I sought help from the Emily Program, a center that focuses on eating disorders. My counselor helped me work through my emotions, gave me tools to use instead of using food, and helped me make parallels with Mike's addiction.

It is coincidental that Mike ended up with struggles similar to the ones I had. When my boys were young, I tried to instill in them a sense of positive self-worth and build up their self-esteem. I told them how good they were inside. When they made mistakes, I encouraged them to see how they could use it in a positive way. I loved on them when their feelings got hurt or they felt left out. On the outside Mike had the whole package, and yet, inside, the emotional pain he carried crippled him.

Mike worked hard on his recovery. He worked on each of the twelve steps, did the corresponding assignments, and participated in the group discussions. One of the required assignments was to share their stories. I remember several calls from Mike to tell me how nervous and anxious he was about it. He spent an inordinate amount of time preparing for it and called afterward to tell me how well it went. Once he got rolling, however, it went really well. He was extremely relieved when he was finished.

Mike was deeply moved by the reactions of his peers at P-Tab. It was the first time he was open, honest, and vulnerable in front of them, and they showered Mike with overwhelming love and acceptance afterward. I think that having positive reinforcement from his peers filled a little of the void inside Mike. In the past, he'd covered up his insecurity and low self-esteem and not allowed others to see his true self under his nonchalant attitude, clowning around, and busy schedule. He told me he loved the attention of being a heroin addict because "it's badass." P-Tab was the bonding experience he needed in order to go forward in his recovery. I felt proud; he had fought his fear and anxiety, and he won that round.

Mike was well liked on his unit, and his peers looked up to him. He was gifted with leadership skills and was elected to be the leader of his unit. I could see how the guys easily gravitated toward Mike because of his positive attitude and outgoing personality. He didn't sugarcoat his failures, and I believe that his transparency encouraged his peers. He genuinely cared for others and strived to help them be successful in the program. He took the time to listen to their stories, and he could relate to them. His story was their story, though the drug of choice was different. He didn't judge them because he'd been in their shoes. His unit peers had shared with one another some of the most intimate aspects of their addictions. They all understood one another.

Mike could be as hilarious as he could be serious. One evening, after lights-out, Mike and his roommate snuck out to the storage room at the end of the hallway. They each took out a wheelchair and raced down the hallways as quietly as they could. Mike crashed into a door, which woke up several guys. Soon all of the guys were piled into the wheelchairs and racing around the hallways. The fun lasted until the night attendant caught up with them. The next day Mike had to meet with his counselor, and he took responsibility for the incident. I think Mike lost the privilege of going into town for a couple weeks, but I can still hear the hint of mischievous joy in his voice as he recounted that event.

He had his share of ups and downs at P-Tab, but he was able to work through them. The guys on his unit became very tight. Spending ninety days with mostly the same people allowed time for them to grow close. He didn't share extensively what each day was like, but I could tell by our phone conversations and visits that he was really beginning to understand his addiction and why he used.

Mike looked forward to the unit's weekly outings to the movies, the swimming pool, and even once to Walmart. He called to tell me about each outing. I found it especially funny how positive Mike was about the shopping trips. At home he hated shopping.

On December 3, after his ninety days were complete, Mike moved to West Hills Lodge, a halfway house in Owatonna, Minnesota. Moving there was a step toward living independently while maintaining his sobriety.

I drove to Granite Falls the evening before his move and spent the night at a local motel. In the morning, I drove to P-Tab to pick Mike up. He was packed and ready to go when I arrived, but he had a hard time saying goodbye to his friends and the staff there. He was excited to move forward, yet I sensed he was apprehensive as well. He was leaving the safety and security of the treatment center he'd come to rely on. During the drive, he confirmed that he was very anxious about moving to yet another new living environment. I listened and tried to encourage him in this new adventure.

We stopped for breakfast at a small local restaurant on the way there. He was relatively relaxed and in a talkative mood. We laughed and joked around with each other. I deeply enjoyed my time with Mike that day. I saw the son I knew and loved without the aid of drugs. I had my boy back.

10. The Cycle of Relapse

When we arrived, the house manager was waiting for Mike. Mike needed to read and sign the paperwork before bringing his things in and getting settled. It was a very structured facility.

Structure was an important part of recovery for Mike because when he was using, he was focused on getting and using his heroin. His life was chaotic. Those daily activities that are so ingrained in our lives, like setting your alarm and getting up in the morning, showering, putting on clean clothes, brushing your teeth, and making your bed, as well as preparing meals and taking time to eat, were things that he no longer did on a daily basis. He had a steady diet of fast food, junk food, and handfuls of granola, if he ate at all.

Maintaining his sobriety was task number one. He was required to attend weekly AA/NA meetings in town. He needed to secure a sponsor and work with him on his twelve steps. At the mandatory Monday-evening house meeting, the guys discussed how their sobriety was going and addressed problems or concerns that came up during the week. They did step work or meditation together as well. This was a priority for everyone. When Mike secured a job, he had to make sure it didn't conflict with his Monday-night meeting.

They shared house responsibilities. In addition to keeping their rooms clean and doing their own laundry, the guys took turns cleaning the house each week. The house employed a cook who planned meals and supervised as the residents set the table, cleaned the dining room, and did dishes.

Mike shared a room with one or two other guys during his stay. That was difficult for him, as Mike was a neat freak and his roommates weren't. It caused a few quarrels, but they worked out their differences.

Another requirement was finding employment. Mike got a job at a giant tomato greenhouse just outside town that supplied tomatoes to several local restaurants. His work included planting, watering, and weeding the tomatoes. When the crop was ready to be harvested, he picked, cleaned, and bagged them to be sold to the restaurants. Mike wasn't fond of the job. He came home at day's end cold, wet, and covered in mud. He complained frequently of how hard the work was and how sore his hands, feet, and back were from all the work. But it filled the requirement and helped pay the bills.

Mike's new life in Owatonna went well. He fit in and made good friends through work and AA meetings in town. When we talked with him, he sounded happy. Allan and I drove out to see him as often as his schedule allowed. We'd pick him up at the sober house and go out to dinner, see a movie, or do any shopping he needed.

One frigid Friday evening, Allan drove down to see Mike. Later, he told me,

I stayed at a Microtel not far from West Hills. After I checked in, I drove over to pick up Mike. I went inside and met a few family members who were visiting their children. We went out to eat and then took in the Owatonna Junior Blades hockey game, a league for eighteen- and nineteen-year-olds. While there, I ran into a former coach's family. They were there watching their son play. We spent a few minutes chatting about the Blades. After the second period, I ran into a friend from the Cities whose son was playing. He told me about his son and what he was doing with his life. He asked me why I was there, and I told him my son lived and worked here and we were spending the evening together. The conversation was uncomfortable because I was dancing around the reason why Mike was really here. I was thinking to myself how lucky these guys were to be here, watching their sons play. I was here with my addict son watching a game. You know, under different circumstances, Mike could have been playing hockey on the team. It made me feel really sad to think that.

After the game, I dropped off Mike and went back to my hotel room. On Saturday morning I picked up Mike and we helped a friend of his move into a house. After we finished, Mike, two of his recovering friends, and I drove to a really small lake where they had an icehouse set up. Mike and his friends talked about their recovery, and his friends shared parts of their stories with me while we fished. After it got dark, I left to come home. Boy, did I have a terrible time finding my way off the lake, even with Mike's directions!

You know, the best thing about the weekend was all the time I got to spend with him. I hadn't spent that much

> time with him since he left for Hazelden in July. It was great, the two of us just hanging out and being together. Enjoying each other's company with the typical banter we used to enjoy before his addiction. Man, I had a great time with him.

The 2008 Christmas season was quickly approaching, and we were unsure if Mike would be able to be with us. He was able to get a day pass and drove to the house early Christmas morning to spend a few hours together as a family. He arrived later than we'd planned, and Allan was sitting by the window, waiting and worrying that he might not show up or, worse, show up high. But Mike arrived clean and sober and excited to spend the day with his family. I hadn't thought it would really happen. I was overjoyed to have Mike home, even for a few hours. I felt blessed that our family was intact and Mike was in recovery.

On a Saturday in early January 2009, we planned a day trip to Wisconsin, a two-and-a-half-hour drive away, for my family's Christmas celebration. Mike got a day pass from West Hills and planned to drive the sixty miles from Owatonna to Saint Paul and meet us at our house that morning. The night before the trip, a blizzard hit, and at one point the highways were closed. Everyone was anxious that this trip might have to be canceled. The next morning Allan checked the highway conditions and found out the highways were opened. Our trip was on.

Mike left Owatonna at 8:00 a.m. Because of the slow road conditions, we met Mike late that morning in a parking lot in Woodbury, a city fifteen miles east of Saint Paul.

He jumped into our car, and off we went. It was a very slow drive to my dad's place. Dan navigated the treacherous roads into Wisconsin safely, and we arrived midafternoon instead of midmorning. Since Mike had a 6:00 p.m. curfew, we spent less than two hours with my family, opening gifts and eating a quick meal before heading back. The road conditions had improved, so the trip back was faster. We dropped Mike off at his car, and he drove back to Owatonna. He arrived fifteen minutes late. He was unsure if there would be a consequence for his tardiness. But he didn't care about that: he was so happy to spend time with family that he'd take any consequences. Fortunately, West Hills didn't enforce any.

Mike left West Hills Lodge in spring 2009 and moved back home with us. I was thrilled to have Mike at home, but at the same time it was hard to have him there. I refrained from asking questions about how he was doing. He went to AA meetings and hung out with his sober friends. It wasn't the structure he was accustomed to, but for a time it worked.

Then I sensed that something wasn't quite right with Mike. Call it a mother's instinct. He seemed off. He was spending more time away from home with "friends," coming home early in the morning and sleeping late into the day. He was evasive when I asked him questions. I was suspicious of the changes in his behavior, and yet I couldn't pinpoint anything specific. Allan and I talked about this change, but once again, we either didn't get it or subconsciously ignored the obvious.

Mike relapsed in April 2009. He had been sober for seven months. He made arrangements to enter a thirty-day lockdown treatment program, this time at the old St. Mary's/Riverside Hospital close to the University of Minnesota campus. Mike's fourth-floor room had a great view of the Mississippi River. Just like his previous two inpatient treatments, this one went well. Mike thrived in the treatment setting. I think he felt safe in the environment the treatment center provided because he wasn't able to use or get drugs. He could share his story freely without feeling guilt and shame because everyone there was chemically dependent. They all shared a special camaraderie.

On one visit, Mike introduced us to some of the female residents he had met. It seemed he had charmed them with his usual charisma.

"Mom, this is Rhonda and Shelly. They have been here a little longer than me."

"Nice to meet you both. How is it going for you?"

"It's okay," Rhonda replied as she shrugged her shoulders. "I've been in treatment before. Same ole shit."

Shelly wrapped her arm through Mike's. "This kid really helps lighten up the place. He keeps us laughing with his jokes."

"Well, that doesn't surprise me at all. He makes us laugh with his lame jokes too."

"We like it when he comes down to our room and sits with us. He can tell a bullshit story that makes us all crack up."

"That lasts until the staff warden pops in and chases him out," Rhonda said with a frown.

I looked at Mike with raised eyebrows and rolled my eyes. He produced a sheepish grin.

"Seriously, though, Mike is a great guy. You have a really sweet son."

"Thanks, we think so too."

"He's really trying to get this twelve-step stuff, which isn't easy at all. I'm on my third treatment center, and it's really hard to keep going over and over these same steps. One day maybe I'll get it."

"Oh, sure you will. One day. Maybe." Mike winked at them. "See you ladies later. We're heading to my room for the rest of our visit."

"Bye; it was nice to meet you," I called over my shoulder as I followed Mike.

I remember sitting with him in his room on his bed. He was talkative and smiling, and his eyes were clear. He seemed happy, like his old self. I could tell he loved being in treatment where he felt secure.

Before Mike's inpatient treatment, he and Allan had planned a forty-mile Iron Man bike ride. Since Mike was in treatment, he was unable to ride. Allan explained,

> Mike and I had done this bike ride April 2008, and even then he had a hard time completing the ride. He complained he was tired when I got him up. He wanted something to eat while we were en route, and then he had to stop to use the bathroom frequently during the ride. What I was unaware of was that Mike was using heroin at that time. I just thought he was hungover from a night of partying.
>
> This year, since Mike was back in treatment, he was unable to do the ride with me. I had no ill will toward him. I felt sorry he had been using and was back in rehab. But Linda

> and I were not going to let this relapse interrupt our lives. We weren't going to stop doing what we wanted to be doing because of Mike's relapse. That would be codependency.

I, too, was sad that Mike was back in treatment, but I understood that was where he needed to be. I willingly rode in Mike's place, even though I had not been actively training for the ride. It was good to be out with Allan doing something other than focusing on Mike and his addiction. The ride was cold and windy, and it rained most of the way. We stopped after twenty miles, went home, showered up, and visited Mike.

Mike was released at the end of May. He came home and went back to work. He relapsed again in June.

After this relapse, Allan and I decided that Mike could not continue to live with us. We didn't feel afraid or worry that Mike would hurt us, but it was emotionally and mentally draining because we were never sure if he was sober or not. It kept us on edge. He stayed out late and disrupted our sleep when he came home. Of course, I worried that he was using when he was out, and I was scared he would get heroin laced with some other drug and overdose. My mind ran on a hamster wheel with all those what-ifs.

I've read and heard from others in the recovery community that relapse is a part of recovery, although there are different schools of thought on it. My personal understanding of the role of relapse grew as I watched Mike cycle through many.

According to the website Addictions and Recovery, relapse is a process; it's not an event. There are three stages of relapse: emotional, mental and physical. Both the emotional and mental stages can happen weeks or months before the event of physical relapse. It's important to understand the early warning signs of relapse and specific relapse prevention techniques for each stage of relapse.[11]

Mike knew about relapse prevention and what he needed to do in order to stay substance free. Sometimes he was able to implement a plan, but at other times his plan went out the window as his cravings for heroin overtook him. He was using more often, and his tolerance was increasing, so he needed more heroin than before to get the same high. His funds were limited, and even now, I don't know how he was purchasing his drugs. Each relapse was harder for him to recover from, not only due to the physical need for heroin, but also from the mental and emotional toll it took on him.

Mike talked to me about the tremendous amount of shame and guilt he felt after each relapse. While we often think of them as similar, these two words mean very different things. According to Merriam-Webster.com, *shame* is "a condition of humiliating disgrace or disrepute." *Guilt* is defined as "feelings of deserving blame especially for imagined offenses or from a sense of inadequacy." The difference between shame and guilt is simple:

Shame = ***You*** are bad/disgraceful/wrong

Guilt = Your ***behavior*** is bad/wrong/disgraceful

Mike felt both conditions acutely. He transferred that perception to us, thinking that we were as disappointed in him as he was with himself. That was never the case. We were sad about his addiction, but we never blamed him for it, nor were we disappointed in him. That was something I wish that Mike had really understood.

I was fearful and worried each time he relapsed. I was very afraid that Mike might die from his addiction. I just didn't think how I would ever get over losing him.

Mike always called me when he relapsed. He didn't want to talk to Allan or his brothers. Allan has always said that I developed a strong bond with each of my sons. Each of them will call me before talking to him.

Mike and I could discuss anything, especially his drug issues. We'd had a close relationship from the time he was a little boy, when Mike would tell me things that most kids wouldn't tell their moms. The depth of our communications only intensified as Mike got further into his disease. I think he knew I wouldn't judge him or shame him. I was in his corner, fighting for him. And Mike knew he had my unconditional love. Allan had the same love for Mike, and he would fight for him just as I would, but I think Mike felt that his dad would judge him more harshly. Allan had been the disciplinarian when the kids were growing up: as a stay-at-home mom, I would talk to Allan about their behavior or disobedience, and then he would be the one to dole out the consequences after work. If there was an issue or problem, the boys would usually come to me first, and I would be a kind of buffer for them when they talked to Allan. I think Mike felt like a huge disappointment and therefore was ashamed to talk to his dad, initially, about his relapses.

Mike made arrangements to live in a halfway house in Saint Paul. Since he'd been in treatment three times already, he stated that he knew what he needed to do. His plan was to "work his program." He lived there for several months, staying sober, and after that we allowed him to move back in with us, despite our earlier decision in June.

On Mike's twenty-first birthday, we celebrated at the Chatterbox Pub, a local restaurant in Saint Paul, with Sean, Dan, Holly (Dan's girlfriend), and Jon, a close family friend. Jon has been like a son to Allan and me. He has been a part of our family and family celebrations for many years. Jon lived behind us when he and Dan were three or four, and they became good friends. Over the years, he grew close to Sean and eventually became a close friend of Mikey's as well.

The next holiday we celebrated was Christmas. The five of us joyfully toasted Mike's presence with us with hot cider. It took most of the morning to open Christmas presents as we savored the time together as a family. We feasted on a delicious turkey dinner in the afternoon. Mike was sober. We had much to be grateful for that day.

In spring 2010, Mike relapsed once again. He contacted his health insurance, which approved another twenty-eight-day treatment program at Hazelden, this time at the adult facility in Center City, Minnesota. Once again, Mike did well and loved being in that environment, making many friends on his unit. He worked hard on his recovery and made progress on his twelve steps, getting through steps five and six, I think, during that time. Then he was admitted into the ninety-day aftercare unit called Jellinek, also at Hazelden. It was there that he met Max, who became his close friend.

Mike and Max hit it off right away. Max was older than

Mike and had been a sniper in the marine corps. Max was athletic, intelligent, and a "trust-fund baby," using Mike's words. The two of them spent much of their free time working out at Hazelden's state-of-the-art exercise center and running on the many trails that weave throughout the grounds. This was the first time Mike was interested in taking care of his body and pushing it to its limits, and during treatment he became extremely physically fit—or, in his words, "very buff."

As an addict, it's easy to go from one addiction to another. This is called cross addiction or addiction transfer, in which you develop another type of addiction or engage in a compulsive behavior that triggers the brain's dopamine reward center.[12] People in early recovery from alcohol or drugs are more susceptible to cross addiction because their brains are still looking for that feel-good dopamine rush they got when they were using. Physical fitness can become an addiction, and Mike's counselors kept a watchful eye on him, even at one point having Mike cut back on workouts, which irked him to no end. True to Mike's nature, he and Max sneaked a few extra workouts in.

Max finished his time at Hazelden before Mike did and relocated to Carbondale, Colorado, thirty miles northwest of Aspen, as part of his aftercare plan. He encouraged Mike to move out there too because, he said, the sober opportunities there were endless. The more Mike talked with Max, the more moving there seemed like a good fit for him.

About two weeks before Mike was to be discharged, he called home midmorning. I recognized the number and picked up the phone right away.

"Yo, yo, Mommadukes, whazz up?"

"Nothing much. Sup with you, dawg?" We bantered back and forth for a couple minutes.

Then he asked, "Is Dad home? Can you put him on too?"

"He is. Just a sec."

A minute later Allan joined with a "Hey, buddy. What's up?"

"I have something I want to discuss with you two."

"Okay, what's that?" I asked.

"I'm thinking of moving to Carbondale, Colorado. It's not far from Aspen. They have a great recovery community."

We were stunned by this news.

"Hmm, what brought this about?" Allan asked.

"You know Max—you met him a couple times—he's moved out there. He's been talking to me about it. I think it might be a good fit for me."

"Ah. Wow! This is a surprise," Allan replied. "Do we need to talk now about it? I think Mom and I need some time to think about this. Can we talk more on Sunday when we visit you?"

"Sure, no problem. I am really considering it, though."

"Mike, I understand, but it's coming out of the blue for us. We need some time to let this sink in."

"Mom, I know that. That's why I'm giving you a heads-up."

"Good. I appreciate that a lot."

"Hey, I gotta go. Group time is coming up in a few. Love you."

"Okay, love you too," Allan and I said in unison.

I could hear the dial tone as I stared at the phone in my hand.

"Is he serious?" I asked.

"I sure don't know. Where did that come from? Seems like it's out of left field."

"I guess we'll hear more from him on Sunday."

I started to process this idea of Mike's. I wasn't sure about having Mike so far away from us or from me. Yet, it might be a good counter to his pattern of relapsing. He would be my first child to leave the state. My momma's heart ached with the sadness of that. Still, I thought it might just be the right next thing for him to do.

Sunday came slowly that week. We drove the forty-five minutes out to visit him. I had made chocolate chip cookies for him and brought him a few personal items he'd requested. We stood as the staff looked through our items to make sure there was no contraband and then waited for him to come down from his room. When he arrived, he gave us hugs and gladly accepted the things we'd brought. We went to his room and talked more about the move. Mike was really excited about the possibility.

"I think this will be a really good move for me," he said. "I've been talking with my counselor. She thinks that I need to get out of the Twin Cities because it's just too easy for me to fall into my old patterns. There's an intern from Carbondale, Brendon, doing his clinician work here. He works at Jaywalker Lodge, an addiction treatment continuum. He says the men there are highly motivated to recover. We've been talking about the opportunities out there. He told me about a St. Paul Sober Living residence there as well. Brendon said it's a recovery-centric community and there are a lot of people my age living in Carbondale."

"Have you talked to Max? How's he liking it out there?"

"I have. He told me he thinks I'll love it. The community is so supportive of him. There are AA and NA meetings. He's meeting a lot of people in recovery. I can find a sponsor there too."

"How are you feeling about being so far away from home? Mom and I and your brothers are so close here."

"I think it will be a new beginning for me—a clean slate, where I can start over. I need to get away from here, where it's so easy for me to relapse. I think Dan and Sean will be okay with it. They can come and visit me."

"What about employment opportunities?"

"Max thinks I can find a job pretty easily. There's a grocery store, a couple convenience stores, an auto mechanic shop, and a couple hotels. I think I will be able to find a job."

"Have you thought about when you might move there?"

"I'm thinking right when I get out of Hazelden. I can come home for a few days, get my things together, and drive out there."

"Mike," Allan said, "I think this might be a really good opportunity for you. Mom and I want the best for you. We want you to live a sober life. If you think it will be too hard to stay here, I'll support your moving."

I said, "Honestly, I don't want you to move away, but I think it might be a good move for you. I do want you to stay away from heroin and stop your relapses. If you hit a bump in the road here, you could end up using and in treatment again. I sure don't want that for you, and I'm sure neither do you. I want you to think long and hard about this move. I will support whatever decision you make."

"Thanks, Mom. That's what I'm thinking. Plus, I don't want to put you guys or myself through this again. I want to stay clean and sober."

Allan said, "You have a couple more weeks before you have to make your decision. Why don't you continue talking to your counselor about your aftercare plan. Like Mom said, I will support whatever decision you make. I want you to be as successful as you can, and if moving to Carbondale will do that, I'm all for it."

"I know you do, Dad. That sounds good to me too."

Over the next couple weeks, Mike continued to talk about relocating to Colorado. We met with his counselor and Brendon prior to Mike's discharge to help formulate his aftercare plan. We all agreed that this move would be a positive step for Mike and, in the long run, help break the cycle of relapse and keep him on the course of recovery. Max's presence was another incentive. Mike decided to go ahead with the move.

11. Like a Kid in a Candy Store

In June, Mike packed his car and headed to Carbondale. Allan drove out there with him. They arrived midafternoon, after eighteen hours on the road. Allan says he remembers two distinct things: the sadness he saw in me as I watched my youngest son drive off at sunset, heading west, and the joy in Mike's face the day after they arrived in Carbondale, when he and Max rode their mountain bikes up Mushroom Rock State Park and back. Mike wiped out four times, twice over the top of the handlebars, and he had road rash up and down his side, and yet he smiled like a kid in a candy store.

The heaviness in my heart lifted as Allan told me about Mike and Max's bike ride. I could picture Mike jetting up and down the mountain like a crazy man and his giddy pleasure in wiping out. Mike was in his element. Even though he was fourteen hundred miles away, I had the excited feeling that this was the beginning of a new chapter in his life.

Mike made a life in Carbondale that we knew very little about during those early months. We didn't hear a lot from him at first; he was busy getting settled, going to AA meetings, and looking for a job. It wasn't until after his death that we learned about his impact on this small town. Brendon later told me, "One of the first things I noticed about Mike was his core kindness and the positive way he interacted with his peers and staff. I tried to plant seeds about him coming to Carbondale. When I came back to Jaywalker in September, Mike had fully integrated into this community."

One of Mike's new connections in Carbondale was Kelly, who attended AA meetings at a local center. After Mike's death, he shared his memories of Mike with me:

> The meeting is called Focus 164 and is a reading of the Big Book followed by discussion. The residents of the sober house were required to attend this meeting each week. Mike became an active member right away. He asked me to sponsor him after two weeks because of my passion for the solution provided in the Big Book. I remember that he was a sponge about how to stay sober and acquiring a spiritual awakening. My first impression of Mike was how likable he was with everyone he met. Being in recovery, I recognized the need to be liked and how we can change who we are depending on the conditions we arrive in. I could see myself in Mike in this way and was attracted to him because he was so likable and fun to be around.

After a few months, Mike got tired of St. Paul Sober Living and moved into a condo in Basalt, a nearby community, with Max and his friend Troy. Mike soon got frustrated with the living situation; dishes were left unwashed, his food would get eaten, and privacy was rare, but the arrangement worked for a while.

Mike also house-sat for Jo and Rob, owners of CrossFit Bonedale, where Mike worked out. They were a real saving grace for Mike. They had no children and treated him like their own son. Mike called them his Colorado parents. He stayed at their ranch and watched their livestock when they were out of town. The love and nurturing that Jo and Rob provided for Mike were amazing. When he got into trouble, they took care of him. When his car needed repairs, Rob took care of it at the auto repair shop he owned. They watched over him and showered him with love. We didn't know them very well, but Rob and Jo contributed in no small part to Mike's long periods of sobriety in Carbondale.

Mike called us frequently, and he mostly talked about all the things he was doing: his AA and NA meetings; the people he met there; and his many activities, including hiking, dirt biking, and CrossFit competitions. CrossFit is a form of interval training, a strength and conditioning workout that is made up of functional movement performed at a high intensity level.[13] The workout program draws on the best aspects of cardiovascular fitness and challenged Mike's athletic development in the same way that hockey had challenged him, and he loved it. CrossFit culture is also known for a particular camaraderie. Team members encourage and support one another in workouts and competitions. Mike succeeded in this intense program, and I think he felt a huge sense of accomplishment as well. It helped increase his self-esteem, especially when he felt bad about himself. For Mike it was a maximum investment with a high return—the perfect metaphor for his life.

He got a job stocking shelves at City Market, a local grocery store. Eventually the store manager noticed that he had a unique ability to work well with customers and employees. Mike moved up the corporate ladder to customer service manager. He loved working with people but did not like the corporate culture nor the need to discipline the people he supervised. Kelly remembered,

> Any relationship requires time to build trust, and sponsorship is no different. With the common disease of addiction, it takes less time to build trust depending on desperation. It took Mike about a month or so to become comfortable talking about his feelings with me. It came about through steps we read through and discussed. During this time Mike got a job at City Market that helped his self-esteem. I helped him with the ups and downs of life through the steps. Being newly employed, he worked all different hours, which wasn't healthy for Mike in early recovery. Working the program helped him understand that it is not life that is the problem but how we react to it. Our age difference at times was a hindrance because Mike didn't think I understood what he was going through. I tried to tell him that he needed to help me understand. We would eventually come to a place of understanding through a common goal.

One of Mike's coworkers at City Market, Brenda, was a recovering alcoholic and addict. They became close nonromantic friends, attending AA meetings and sober events together, and she told me he was instrumental in her recovery. They hiked the surrounding mountains, and he spent holidays at her place. Their friendship was built on honesty and trust, though it would eventually be tested by his relapses.

Mike developed a relationship with a Hispanic customer who worked two jobs to support his family. The man could not afford a car and had to walk to each job, so Mike gave the man his bike. Mike said the man needed it more than he did. Plain and simple. Mike was never into owning stuff. Stuff never tied him down.

Mike was also very good at helping customers, and he made a big impression on them as well. Several of them told me that sometimes they came to the store just to see Mike and get a hug from him. He was more than willing to spend time with people and share his story with them. That's how he met Marcia, who would become his "Colorado grandma." Marcia told me,

> The first time I met Mikey was in City Market in the frozen foods department. He was on a stepstool and turned to ask if I needed anything. I could not help but be blown away by his dark hair and those piercing blue eyes, like none I'd ever seen. His smile was so infectious. I was hooked. We talked several times when I came into the store to shop. He shared that he was being promoted to customer service manager. How perfect he was for that position! Each time I came to the store he would give me a big hug. He told me how I would love his parents and siblings. I must admit that I could have stayed and talked longer each time, for I felt special when he showed his love and concern for my welfare. He was always willing to assist me when I shopped.

Mike once told me that he had been called out by management for being too friendly with the customers. Not long after that, he stopped in front of the store camera and gave Marcia a big hug as he looked directly into the camera. Oh, how he loved telling that story!

In July 2010, Allan, Dan, Sean, and I flew to Seattle to visit my in-laws, Bob and Val, for a long weekend. Mike met us at the airport, and the five of us made the two-and-a-half-hour drive to their house on Puget Sound together. Mike talked often of a memorable afternoon that weekend when he went fishing by the marina entrance and caught a sizable salmon. He cleaned it, and his grandma Val cooked it for dinner that night.

We golfed together, hung out at the beach, and cooked hotdogs over a bonfire. It was a wonderful time we spent as a family. Mike and his brothers hung out on the deck and bantered back and forth like they had done before Mike's addiction. They helped their grandpa Bob with repairs around the house, and in the evenings they played catch with their dad in the backyard. It was so good to see Mike doing well in his recovery. The four of us missed having Mike in Minnesota, but we knew his life in Colorado was helping him stay clean and sober.

All too soon our visit came to an end. I remember saying goodbye to him at the airport and crying as we sat at the gate, waiting to board our plane. How I missed my baby boy already! But we arrived home feeling good about the vacation we'd shared.

In October 2010, Allan and I drove to Colorado to visit Mike. Allan loves road trips. I could hardly wait to see Mikey in his new environment. We arrived in Carbondale around lunchtime, and I called Mike to let him know we'd arrived. I could hear the excitement in his voice as we talked. He told me we should meet him at a park in the middle of town; he had a surprise for us.

As we drove up to the park, I saw Mike waiting with a huge smile on his face. I jumped out of the car just as he got to my door, hugged him tightly, and gave him a kiss. I told him how good it was to see him and how much I'd missed him. He reciprocated and then turned to his dad for a hug.

As they were talking, Max pulled up in his jeep, pulling a trailer loaded with a huge rubber raft. We were going rafting and fishing on the Colorado River! We stopped for sandwiches, chips, and drinks before heading to the river.

Mike was new at fly-fishing and excited to show us his new skill. He and Max fished all afternoon, catching nothing more than a ton of smiles. As the two of them talked, laughed, and shared inside jokes, Allan and I looked on with deep gratitude in our hearts. It's hard to describe the feeling I had watching my son in his new world—so happy, carefree, and sober. I can't say it was worth the harrowing nights of Mike's drug use, but it was a joy to see how far he'd come.

After our fishing excursion, they took us to a local restaurant called the White House for pizza and salad. It was crowded and the atmosphere robust. As we waited for a table, Mike and Max chatted with many of the patrons. I was amazed at the number of people Mike knew and how easily he conversed with them. I shouldn't have been surprised because he was always so outgoing and friendly, but he had amassed so many friends in his short four months there.

Mike had another surprise planned for us the next day. He arrived at our hotel with an impish grin on his face. The three of us piled into the car and headed out. Our first

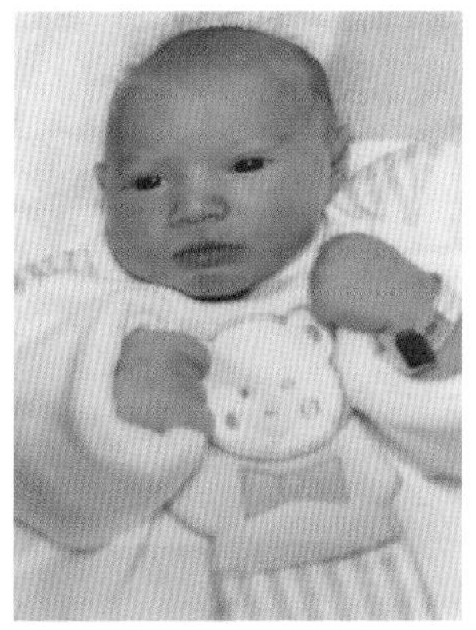

Mike's newborn picture, 8/8/88.

Mike, Dan, and Sean, December 1988.

Sean and Mike having some summertime fun, summer 1991.

Dan, Sean, and Mike, Christmas 2009.

Working out at CrossFit Bonedale, fall 2011.

Mike having some fun with his mom after a grueling workout.

The Boozlers. Back row: Corey, Andy, Keith, Greg, and Anthony; front row: Mike, Ben, and Nick, summer 2006, and Boozlers: recreated picture without Mikey, 2017.

Mikey chillin' on his grand-parents' deck, Birch Bay, Washington, summer 2011.

Mike's big smile after his huge salmon catch.

Mike's catch on the Puget Sound, Washington.

One big happy family: Sean, Jon (our family's good friend), Mikey, Dan, Allan, and me.

Mike's Aunt Candee and Uncle Michael.

Mike and his beloved grampa Red.

The family (Linda's side). Back row: Aunt Harriet, Sean, Betty (my mom), Jon. Middle row: Myself, my dad, and Dan. Front: my sister Tracy.

The Morrison Clan after a round of golf: Mike, Dan, Grampa Bob, Allan, and Sean. Front row: Grandma Val and myself.

Best friends: Brenda and Mikey, 3/22/12.

A boy with his toy, fall 2010.

Mike just being his silly self.

Mike in his super safety hero's costume at City Market, October 31, 2010.

He was the bomb.

Mike with his friend's furry malamutes, Dupree and Ryder, September 2011.

Mike Morrison
"Mikey Mo"

8/8/88 - 6/21/12

One year ago today you left us for a better place. We miss you Mikey - the smile, the jokes, that sweet spirit and that zest for life and adventure. Keep smiling Buddy! See you in heaven. Love, Mom, Dad, Dan and Sean.

The memoriam placed in the Saint Paul *Pioneer Press* for Mike's one-year anniversary.

Mike's final resting place at Acacia Park Cemetery, Mendota Heights, Minnesota.

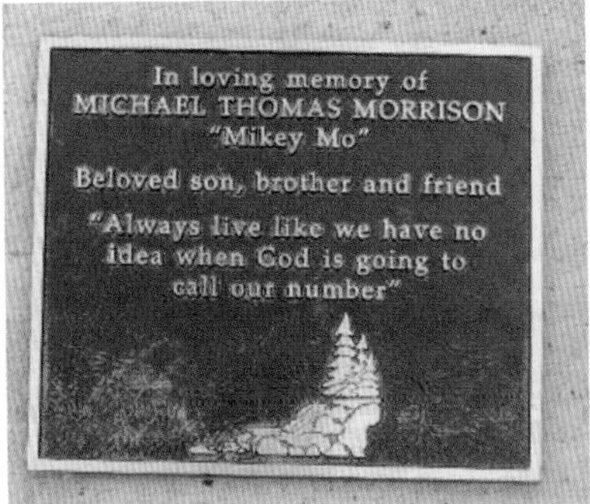

The plaque we had made inscribed with Mike's life motto, placed next to a bench overlooking the Mississippi River, Saint Paul, Minnesota.

Allan took this picture at Blue River State Recreation Area, Milford, Nebraska. We used this pic for Mike's memorial card.

stop was for breakfast at a local diner—Mike loved a big breakfast, especially when someone else was paying for it. As soon as we finished eating, Mike urged us to get on the road. Allan drove, and Mike rode shotgun; I took the back seat, just enjoying this time with Mike.

At last, Mike told us his plan: ziplining. He was excited and nervous. He later told us that he had been afraid the excursion would not turn out like he'd hoped. But it was a truly memorable event!

When we arrived at the address, the office was locked and empty, with no cars in the parking lot. We sat in the car for a few minutes before another car arrived, and then a jeep pulled in with the zipline company logo on the side. We checked in and read and signed waivers stating we were doing this at our own risk. That was a little unnerving.

All participants were given helmets and leather belts with large hooks to secure around our waists. We piled into a van and headed up the mountain. The drive was amazing. The sky was a clear and vibrant blue, and the sun illuminated the hillside. When we arrived at our first zip line, I looked down the hill at the sagebrush and tumbleweeds that I was about to descend into. I felt invigorated by the mountain air. In the distance you could see others zipping down their lines.

The worker showed us how to secure the line to our belts, and then we walked to the launch platform. When I jumped off, my stomach was in knots; I closed my eyes as I flew down the hill. I landed at the end with a thud. The guys sped down the hill one at a time, screaming and laughing the entire way down.

When the last of us had arrived, the worker asked, "Are you up for another zip ride down?"

"Yes!" we yelled in unison.

This time I was more confident and kept my eyes open as I zipped over the mountainside. With each new trip, I felt myself relax more.

Mike was in his element—the riskier the better for him! Once, as I was waiting my turn to go down, Mike plunged off the platform, turned himself upside down, and waved to me. My heart did a flip! On my next turn, Mike tried to goad me into doing the same thing. No way was I doing that! I was surprised to be enjoying this adventure at all, given the fact that I'm afraid of heights and speed.

Our morning flew by, and before we knew it we had reached the bottom of the mountain. Before heading back to our cars, we stopped in the gift shop, where I purchased a T-shirt for myself. I remember Mike and Allan sitting next to each other on the drive back and seeing Mike's infamous smile. I think he was very proud of himself for arranging such a great time for the three of us.

We drove back to town and stopped at Subway for lunch before we dropped Mike off at his place. Allan and I went back to the motel to rest. Later that afternoon, Mike came by the motel and we hung around the room talking. We decided to order Chinese food and take it to Mike's. I wasn't surprised, when we picked up the food, that Mike knew the owners of the restaurant. We ate our delicious dinner with Mike and his roommates while watching *Monday Night Football.*

On Tuesday Mike worked during the day, so Allan and

I enjoyed the fall weather in Carbondale. We sat outside by Roaring Fork River, reading and dozing in the sun, and I did a little shopping in the afternoon. Mike came over after work and took us to a CrossFit gym, where he had made arrangements for me to take a class. First Mike and I ran two miles outside as a warm-up. Then I attended the class while he did his training. Now, I pride myself in being in good physical shape: I run, swim, and do aerobic classes several times a week. This class still kicked my butt. His dad watched us, shaking his head as we worked out. There was no way Allan would try this "workout on steroids," as I fondly refer to it. Afterward, I was exhausted and barely able to lift my legs, and the next day I found myself sore in places I'd never felt before. I was impressed, knowing that Mike did CrossFit on a regular basis.

Wednesday was our last day with Mike. We went out to breakfast, and then Mike suggested a hike up to Mushroom Rock. It's about an hour's hike over a barely recognizable trail strewn with rocks and boulders. While Allan and I started our hike, Mike ran the trail up and back. Then he completed the trail with us.

After lunch, it was time for us to go. It was hard to say goodbye. I knew that he was making a life for himself there. He had demonstrated his ability to move from his hometown to an unknown city and flourish there. Still, leaving him was incredibly difficult. I held him tightly and told him how proud of him I was and how much I loved him. I thanked him for planning all of our fun activities. I cried as we drove to Denver, but I was grateful for the days we had spent with him.

We returned to Saint Paul, where fall turned into winter. Before I knew it, Christmas was at hand. This was our first Christmas without Mike in Minnesota. The four of us were opening gifts when he called. He took time to talk to each one of us and thanked us for the gifts we had sent him. He told us he was spending the day with friends. It was hard not to have Mike home with us, but knowing that he was doing well in Carbondale eased my discomfort.

In January 2011, Allan's sister, Lori, and her friend Brian flew in from Texas for a long weekend. Mike flew home for a short visit that same weekend. He hadn't been home since moving to Colorado. It was a weekend of frigid temperatures, and the Saint Paul Winter Carnival was in full swing. Founded in 1886, the Winter Carnival is a family-friendly community event that brings parades and crowds and vendors to fill the streets of downtown Saint Paul. We enjoyed the lively atmosphere as we looked at the display of ice sculptures, enjoyed food from local restaurants, and milled about in subzero temperatures. It made for a wonderful mini family reunion, and Jon joined us as well. Lori took a picture of the five of us plus Jon standing in our kitchen, smiling and clearly happy to be together. That picture sits on our fireplace mantel as a constant reminder of the love we share, not just that weekend but always and forever.

Mike also spent some time with his high school friends before he left. The next time he called from Colorado, Mike shared with me some unexpected feelings about his visit.

"I enjoyed being home and spending time with you and Dad and Auntie Lori," he said, "but it was hard when I hung out with my boys. Mom, I just don't fit in with my friends anymore. They know about my addiction and going to the different treatment centers, but they think I'm still the same ole Mike. They wanted me to party with them and do the same things we did before I moved away. I'm just not comfortable with doing that anymore. I think it'll be a long time before I come back to visit."

Surprised and sad to hear this, I replied, "I'm sorry it was so hard for you, Mike. I'm sure it's hard to hang out with them when they are still doing the party scene. Maybe you'll have to talk to a couple of them and tell them how you felt."

"Yeah, maybe. It's kinda uncomfortable to think about doing that."

"I'm sure it is. Now you're back there and you can focus on your life in Carbondale. You can cross that road the next time you decide to come home."

"You're right. Thanks for talking to me, Mom. I love you."

"Love you too. Bye."

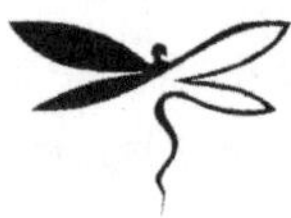

12. A Month of Chaos and Insanity

Prior to his visit home, Mike had begun taking on more responsibilities and adding more activities with his prolonged sobriety. He was working full-time at City Market as the customer service manager. He dealt not only with customer concerns and complaints but also employee work schedules, and he had to discipline employees who didn't show up or broke rules. Mike didn't hire employees, but it was his responsibility to fire them. He hated that part of the job; he did what he needed to but never liked it. He also dealt with management, which was hard for him because he disliked the corporate environment. Mike's bottom line was caring for the people who worked and shopped at City Market. Corporate's bottom line was the almighty dollar. Still, he had to play their game in order to be successful.

He continued his daily CrossFit workouts. He helped instruct new members, especially preteens and teenagers just starting this strenuous regime. On weekends the individual members teamed up for local competitions. Mike would call me, very excited, to share how he'd performed and the overall placement of his team.

He attended AA/NA meetings and events regularly and

sponsored several young men starting out on their recovery journeys. He met with his own sponsor too. In addition to this already busy schedule, in his free time Mike biked and hiked the mountain trails and went camping to hunt deer and elk in the summers. He skied and snowboarded in the winters.

In the spring, Mike added yet another activity to his busy schedule. He decided he wanted to become an EMT. He told me he had been at Target when a customer collapsed near him and paramedics were called to assist. Mike was intrigued as the paramedics jumped into action; he decided right then and there to look into becoming one. On his next day off he went to Colorado Mountain College in Glenwood Springs, a short distance from Carbondale, to learn about the certification requirements. He signed up for the next class. I believe this was the beginning of his ultimate demise.

In his remembrance, Kelly—Mike's sponsor from AA in Carbondale—shared something that I think is important to understanding this time in Mike's life:

> Anybody in recovery will understand the need for a fix through outer events in their life. We don't like to admit it, but this includes the high we get through things like a new partner, a party, a promotion, a new job, money, food, exercise, recognition, or any extreme change in our lives. Mike went through many of these outer highs in the time we had together. After the highs come the lows, followed by guilt and shame. Bill W. calls this emotional sobriety. I shared with Mike that these things weren't bad if taken in moderation or discussed with someone we trust before we

overindulged. Prayer and meditation were the places we found the right answers. But, like myself, he had to find out through pain on his own.

Mike relapsed a few weeks into his EMT training. He had been sober since leaving Hazelden fourteen months earlier, the longest period of time he was clean in his four-year battle with heroin. Mike thrived on constant activity, to the point of physical and mental exhaustion. He never developed the ability to have down time. When he tried to relax, his mind would spin like a hamster on a wheel. He often told me how he would think and rethink about a situation or a conversation he'd had, replaying it in his head over and over. He couldn't shut off his mind. He was always processing what he could have done or said differently.

When he tried to relax, he could reduce his activity level for only short periods of time. Soon he'd feel worried and anxious that he wasn't doing enough and resume his busyness or even add more activities. He'd chide himself for not doing better. Then he'd work longer, faster, harder. This pattern repeated itself, which increased his anxiety level—as well as the craving for heroin.

In the past, Mike had said that he felt normal when he used, that his anxiety dissipated. He could finally relax. The euphoric effect of the heroin enhanced his self-esteem and dulled the feelings of unworthiness that plagued him. His negative feelings melted away and were replaced with feelings of serenity, inner peace, and happiness.

After a few days on heroin, though, the high would end and the positive feelings vanished. The intense shame and guilt of using would pull him further down into the abyss of depression. This cycle repeated, with each relapse longer, faster, and deeper than the previous ones.

This time, the cycle was very bad.

Mike had been living in the lower level of a home owned by Brian, a friend from CrossFit and AA, for the past few weeks after giving up the condo he'd shared with Max and Troy. It is a testament to Mike that Brian trusted him to live in his home with his two kids. But after Mike admitted that he had relapsed, Brian told Mike he needed to find someplace else to live. Brian needed to maintain his own sobriety and protect his daughters from any effects of Mike's relapse.

Mike told Brenda about his relapse and asked if he could move in with her while he looked for a new place to live. Brenda told him that he could move in with her temporarily. What followed was a month of chaos and insanity.

After moving in with Brenda, Mike called to tell me about his relapse. He expressed his angst about taking on too much activity earlier in the year. He was realizing that he could not maintain that pace and stay in recovery. Brenda called me almost daily as well to keep me in the loop on Mike's condition.

It was extremely hard on me to be in Minnesota while Mike relapsed in Colorado. I used my Al-Anon literature and attended a few meetings for moral support and a little sanity, but at the time I didn't fully understand the situation that Mike had put Brenda in.

On April 6, 2011, Mike admitted himself into the Parker Valley Hope (PVH) treatment center in Parker, Colorado. After Mike left for PVH, Brenda wrote a letter to him in her journal about that day and the following few days after he entered treatment again, which she graciously shared with me.

> April 6, 2011: I want to start out telling you how lucky I feel to have such a special person in my life. Mike, you have such an amazing personality, and I'm glad I took the chance to get to know you. I had been a very lost person for a really long time. When you told me you'd relapsed, my heart hurt. I was so worried about you. Today, when you left for treatment, it was really hard for me to say goodbye to you. I hope that you will understand one day how hard it was for me to do what I have done for you. It was recommended that I get my feelings out to you on what I have dealt with and what I will deal with on a daily basis while you are gone. You told me not to tell you anything that happens, that you need time for yourself to get better, and I understand that 100%. However, I have to still deal with my life and yours (work wise) on a daily basis. What you have done the past week has affected me so much! I don't even know how to put all my feelings into words. I hate myself for taking you to Denver [to buy drugs]. I hate myself for letting you use in my house. I hate that I came home one day and you had your shit all over the place. I feel like I lost my best friend and that you are going to push me so far away for letting you do your shit here and me helping you to get it. You know how hard it was for me while we were in Denver. Mike, I have dealt with so much shit in my life and am proud of myself for staying as strong as I did with you, but I'm not as strong inside as I make myself out to be. And I want you to know that I am super pissed that you ate all my chips.

4/9/11—Dawn, from work, called me this morning wanting to know where the store keys are. She wanted me to call you to see where they are. I miss my best friend!! I cherish your friendship like you can't imagine!! The dogs keep going to your door and smelling to see if you're in there or something. You also put a hole in the wall by the TV with the doorknob. Rex came by to pick up your car. I asked him to call me. I wanted to know if he knew if you had anything [drugs] left at the house. He called to say that you seemed pretty serious about not doing that shit anymore and I shouldn't worry about that. Later I texted him to look through your car to be sure nothing was left.

4/10/11—I asked Jordan to come over today and to go through your stuff to make sure you didn't have anything left. I haven't had a real cigarette since the day you left. I finally cleaned out the refrigerator today, and this is everything I found: mango pork, chicken and green beans, shrimp soup along with the goodies, the most shriveled zucchini I have ever seen, and lots of rotten veggies. I felt like puking.

4/11/11—I started my day out crying for absolutely no reason at all. I really wish I could figure this shit out. It isn't getting any easier telling people that you just need a break, knowing where you actually are right now. I miss having you here to talk about stuff. I hate lying to people. . . . I hope you are doing better today.

4/12/11—Jordan came into the store in the afternoon and asked how I was doing; I explained to him the rumors that I had heard today, and he's like, well, then no one knows what's going on if they think he was drinking . . . he was

> doing heroin. Later Deb came in and asked if I've talked to you at all and how you were doing. I told her you were fine, just relaxing and trying to figure stuff out. I told her you had a thirty-day leave of absence but I wasn't sure if you were coming back. You have no idea how much this is wearing on me. I wish it would all go away and people would stop asking me shit. I come home every day and cry.

Once again, I had high hopes for Mike as he went back into treatment. I am ever the optimist. I wanted him to beat this addiction and knew that he could, if he would use the tools he had learned. Back home, I struggled to maintain my equilibrium. I used the tools I learned in Al-Anon: doing my daily meditations, working on the steps, and getting to meetings. But it wasn't easy.

13. A Spiritual Perspective

Mike was relieved to be back in treatment. At PVH Mike met a counselor, Sammy, whose influence would change Mike's view of addiction through the mind and ego. Sammy encouraged Mike to embrace spirituality—a piece of the twelve steps that Mike seemed to be missing.

Sammy was twenty-two years sober when he met Mike. Their first meeting was in a group setting soon after Mike arrived. Sammy recalled walking into the small group and seeing Mike sitting in a chair and flexing his muscles, wearing a soccer jersey and his Yankees baseball cap. Sammy recounted that first meeting to me:

> "Mike was trying so hard to be cool," I said, laughing. I baited Mike: "So, you're a big Yankees fan?"
>
> "Nope, I'm not!" Mike said, giving me a steely look.
>
> I told him, "I suggest you remove your cap and drop the attitude!" But Mike just continued to flex his muscles.

From that conversation I got the sense that Mike was challenging Sammy in front of his peers. I don't know how the rest of that meeting went; Sammy later told me that Mike showed up outside his office door many times after that first meeting, wanting to talk about sobriety, recovery, and sometimes just life in general.

Sammy really appealed to Mike's twentysomething age group. Using Eckhart Tolle's book *The Power of Now,* a spiritual self-help guide focused on releasing pain and finding inner peace, Sammy led his groups through Tolle's approach of responding from deep consciousness and flow, with ease and joy in life. This is intended to lead to fulfillment of purpose, achievement of goals, and a desire to create a better world while fulfilling your inner purpose. Tolle opens the book by sharing the circumstances and experiences leading to his "enlightenment" and its natural enemy, the mind. Like many others, he suffered from anxiety and suicidal depression for many years. I think that Tolle's philosophy helped Mike understand more about himself and his thought patterns. Mike found this journey thrilling, and he gravitated toward Tolle's means of connecting to the indestructible essence of our being: "Being is the eternal, ever-present One Life beyond the myriad forms of life that are subject to birth and death. However, Being is not only beyond but also deep within every form as its innermost invisible and indestructible essence."[14] These lofty thoughts and ideas were way beyond my understanding. I think Mike knew that as well because when he talked to me about them, my response was "Oh really?" or "I don't get that at all." That was okay with me. If it was working for him, that's all that mattered.

At PVH Mike danced his way into many hearts with

his wit, charm, smile, and those amazing blue eyes. Jennifer, a fellow patient who met Mike in his first couple days at Parker Valley, forged a connection with him over their study of Tolle's books. She recalled:

> I met Mike in April 2011. I asked who in rehab was familiar with *The Power of Now* and was told a few people were—Aaron and Mike. When I approached Mike, his smile was the first thing I noticed. I told him I was looking for someone familiar with Eckhart Tolle's teachings, and he got really excited because up until that point, no one had come into rehab already knowing it. Sammy had been introducing people to it, but I already had four years of it. It was my spirituality. It kept me grounded. When I let go of it, I eventually drank. I needed to get back to it, and I knew I needed to be around like-minded people. Mike's excitement and enthusiasm helped me with this. Between him and Sammy, I bounced back quickly. I'm not sure I would have otherwise. The Universe put me in the perfect place at the perfect time. I was placed in Sammy's small group with Mike right beside him. . . . I encouraged him to read Tolle's next book—*A New Earth*—but he had no way to get it. I had read it six times already and had it on my Kindle, which I had with me. I don't share my Kindle with others, as it is my most prized possession. My intuition told me to loan my Kindle to Mike so he could read it. That is so unlike me. I hardly knew Mike. Things were being stolen left and right. My glasses were stolen. And here I was, loaning my Kindle to him. He was so excited. He devoured that book. One day later on, he went to a used bookstore in town. It was only open one day each week. Mike went that day, and wouldn't you know it, they had a copy of *A New Earth*. He was so thrilled! He came back to rehab and

ran up to me to show me! What are the odds they would have that book? His excitement was contagious. (And you sent me that book after he died. I will keep it forever.) We would sometimes talk for hours about consciousness and awakening. We had to be careful because we were opposite sexes and the staff would get suspicious of our motives. He would find something that excited him and hunt me down so he could talk to me about it. It would be an hour later, and we wouldn't even realize we'd been talking that long. Sometimes, he'd knock on the door to my room and chat with my roommate and me even though it was against the rules. Who cared? We were two older women. We weren't going to do anything with a young man like Mike. He made my stay in rehab so much more enjoyable. I didn't want him to go! His sobriety date was the same as mine.

It seemed Mike really had it this time. He was on fire. I was cautious in thinking he had it, though. I'd been through this all before. But he'd been through it more times than I had and was confident, so I was hopeful.

Mike called his dad and me frequently while at PVH to keep us informed of his progress. After his twenty-one-day stay he returned to Carbondale, where he resumed his activities. He told us he was feeling emotionally healthy and looked forward to going back to work, his friends, and his sober life. He was welcomed back by his work friends and AA family.

He and Sammy continued their mentorship/friendship. Mike made the two-hour drive from Carbondale to Denver twice a month to see him. Sammy understood the challenges Mike was facing as he worked on his recovery and had a unique style of challenging Mike in a caring way that fostered that work. After sessions, the two of them went out to dinner, drove around the city, or spent time at Sammy's house visiting with his wife and playing with his toddler daughter. I strongly believe this relationship was one of the main reasons Mike was able to stay clean for the next nine months. The closeness they developed led to them joking about being "brothers from another mother."

Hearing from Mike about how well he was doing always put a smile on my face and a bounce in my step. My days were less stress-filled, and I could go about my daily activities with a lighter heart. Life was starting to settle into a more normal routine once again.

In May 2011 I flew to Colorado to attend a two-week spiritual retreat in Buena Vista. Over Memorial Day weekend, I drove the two and a half hours to Carbondale to see Mike. I arrived Friday afternoon and checked in to my hotel. When I walked into my room, I saw a bouquet of beautiful flowers sitting on the table. Mike called me on his break, and I thanked him for sending them. He told me he'd sweet-talked the front desk receptionist into letting him in the room to drop them off. It was such a loving surprise.

After work, Mike picked me up and took me to dinner with Brenda at the White House. We had a very pleasant meal, and I didn't observe any discord between the two of them. Any trauma from Mike's relapse seemed to have been resolved.

We called it an early evening, and Mike told me he had

a surprise for me the next day . . . but I needed to be up by 5:00 a.m. and dress in clothes that could get dirty. I was pretty skeptical about waking up that early, not for my sake but because Mike had never been an early riser. Sure enough, he rapped on my door at five on the dot.

"Ready to go, Mom?" he asked, a mischievous smile on his face.

"Yep, I am," I said, somewhat apprehensive about this mysterious outing.

"Okay, I hope you're ready for an adventure."

I followed him outside. He walked up to a truck and trailer and opened the back to show me two four-wheelers. His infectious smile stirred excitement inside me. He was taking me off-roading! He drove us about fifteen miles into the hills, parked off the road, and began unloading the vehicles. It was a beautiful, sunny day with a slight breeze.

Unfortunately, Mike couldn't get one of the four-wheelers started. But that didn't dampen his spirit. He had me hop on with him, and off we went. We drove a good eight to ten miles deep into the mountain trails. The scenery was stunning. He drove up and down hills, through riverbeds and pastures, further and further into the wild. Mike wanted so badly to show me an elk, but we never did see any. Eventually I needed to pee. He drove up a long, steep hill and he let me off to go while he turned the machine around. He drove up the hill a bit further to turn it around.

As I finished going, I looked up just in time to see the four-wheeler flip over sideways and roll twice as Mike leaped off.

I screamed, "Mikey!!" and raced up the hill.

I reached him as he was getting up off the ground. He dusted off his jeans, uninjured, and then looked at the vehicle in dismay. It was lodged sideways against a tree, the windshield cockeyed, handlebars bent, and engine humming. "Damn it!" he exclaimed.

He turned the motor off and sat on the wheel. It was eerily quiet. I was too stunned to say anything. After a few minutes, Mike got up and surveyed the damage. He tried to right the four-wheeler, but it didn't budge. He looked in the storage pocket and found one tool.

"Ah shit," he muttered.

Mike toyed with the machine, trying to restart it, but nothing happened. I stood off to one side and started praying. I prayed for patience for him as he worked to start the four-wheeler. I hoped it would be sooner rather than later. We were without our cell phones. We had no food or water and only the one tool. In addition, Mike needed to be at work by noon. Walking out from where we were would take several hours.

Mike continued to tinker. He located the winch and hooked one end to a sturdy tree. I had my camera with me, so I recorded Mikey as, slowly, he pulled it away from the tree and got it right side up.

Next he had to repair the gear, which was stuck in reverse. I stayed out of his way, knowing he needed to concentrate.

"Oh, fuck" was the next phrase I heard from him. It wasn't going well. I continued to pray and kept my mouth shut.

Nearly an hour later, with a few more choice words out of my son's mouth, I heard a click and then *VAROOM*. Success! Relief was etched on his face. Within minutes we were headed back to civilization.

After he'd reloaded the vehicles on the trailer and gotten us back on the road, he said, "Mom, I'm so glad you didn't freak out up there."

"Oh I did, Mikey. I just tried to hide it."

"I really expected you to start crying or yelling at me, especially when I was swearing."

"I prayed! It seems your higher power was sure with us today."

Mike smiled. "Yeah, God has been doing that a lot lately."

14. Dear Heroin

In October 2011, Allan and I drove out to see Mike. He knew we were arriving but didn't know what time. We stopped at City Market to surprise him. When Mike saw us, his face lit up. He said he would come to the motel during his break. He stopped by with Subway over his lunch break.

The next day Mike met us for breakfast. As we walked around town with him, we were amazed at the number of friends he had. On every block, he stopped to talk to someone he knew. He took us to City Market, and people came out of the woodwork to greet him and meet us. They told us what a wonderful son we had and how much they enjoyed working with him. He took us to a farmers market, where he ran into an old guy he knew from working at City Market. Those two sat around talking about old coins and conspiracy theories. I commented to Allan how knowledgeable Mike seemed. Allan said it was one-third truth and two-thirds bullshit. That was so Mike.

That evening Mike took us on a drive to Marble, Colorado, a town in the mountains where marble boulders naturally litter the area. We were at the top of a one-lane road in the middle of nowhere when a four-wheeler appeared ahead of us, going the opposite way. We stopped to talk with the couple riding it, and it turned out they knew Mike from the store. That's how it was with Mike: he made friends everywhere he went.

A couple evenings later we had dinner up at the ranch with Jo and Rob. As Mike showed us the ranch and described everything he cared for while they were out of town, I could tell he loved being there. It was secluded and very quiet. They had two huge malamutes that Mike loved as well. This couple taking Mike under their wings was another answer to our prayers.

After dinner Mike drove us to a secluded spot that he liked, just down the road from the ranch. It was very dark out. We got out of the car and lay on the hood to look at the stars. It was a beautiful sight. Mike said that he and his best buddy, Jordan, would come here to gaze at the stars and ponder life.

I will always remember that field of millions of stars. I felt I could almost reach up to grasp one. I sensed something or someone greater than myself up there, looking down on us. As we lay there in silence, staring at the sky, I felt completely at peace.

The next day we drove into the mountains again so that Mike could shoot his shotgun, which we had brought for him from home. He did his best at shooting at tin cans and rocks. Unfortunately, he couldn't hit a thing.

The following afternoon we drove Mike to Glenwood Springs for dinner at a local Mexican restaurant, and afterward he went to an AA meeting while Allan and I walked around downtown. It's a sleepy little town in the fall and winter, but when summer comes, it's full of tourists who enjoy fishing, hiking, and whitewater rafting.

All too soon our time with Mike came to an end. It had been a great visit, and we felt very comfortable leaving him as we drove back to Minnesota. He was doing well.

This was the second-longest stretch when Mike was clean and sober—nine months from May 2011 to January 2012—and I was grateful for it. Mike and I talked and texted often during this time. When I knew he was doing well, I felt relaxed, I slept better, and I no longer spent my nights worrying about him. When we talked, he sounded happy, content, and like he was enjoying his sobriety.

I recently found a letter Mike wrote to heroin as part of his recovery. I believe he wrote it sometime around the end of 2009 or early 2010, but Mike rarely dated any of his writings. I find his idea of breaking up with his drug of choice very poignant.

Mike lived sober for a few more months. He seemed happy. He was busy with work, AA meetings, and CrossFit workouts and competitions. He spent time on the ski slopes and met with Sammy regularly. We were grateful for these months of Mike's recovery. We texted or spoke often during these precious times with our son. Looking back now, having that time was a gift.

Dear Heroin-

We have had some great times together. Remember the first time we met, Nick introduced us in his car? That was a great time, that is something I won't be able to ever forget. All the times we hung out, had sleepovers and pulled all nighters together were amazing. I even found ways to sneak off away from work to see you, damn was I sneaky. You taught me to lie my way out of many situations, situations that I was in because of you to begin with. You also taught me how to steal, not just physical, material items but feelings and trust. All the physical things that I took so I could be with you don't add up to all the feelings, wants and needs I stole from people in the process. Being able to return the items or cash is so easy, but regaining the trust and friendships, thats something that I'm going to really have to work at. If you still haven't noticed, there is a problem with us being together. I'm not willing to give up all my relationships, fun, hobbies, feelings or life just for you. I want to be able to have fun without you, to be able to play hockey, ice fish, hunt, read, write, smile, care, and feel. So, this letter is to let you know that I don't want to see you any more. Thanks for the good times, but I'm done w/ them now. I hope I never see you again.

-Mike

Part Two

Part Two
Part Two
Part Two
Part Two
Part Two
Part Two

15. Two Calls

Although things had seemed good during our visit in October, Mike was already on shaky ground. Jennifer recalled, "In late September and early October 2011, Mike's attendance at Sammy's group began to slow. Mine wasn't great, either." Sammy's support group brought together many who were in recovery from the surrounding community, plus those who had recently finished their time at PVH, to work on spirituality, a major component of AA. It was held at PVH even though it was not part of their aftercare program. Jennifer continued,

> In late October I pulled up and found Mike not there. When I walked up to the group and asked Sammy where he was, Sammy shook his head. I thought he meant Mike was using again. I began to cry and shake. He meant Mike hadn't called or anything. He didn't know his status. Sammy asked me to try and contact him. I texted and called him. He wouldn't speak to me, but he did text me for a while. I used our common spirituality to get him back. I convinced him to call Sammy. It wasn't easy. He was stubborn! He did come back, though. For a few months, we had the pleasure of Mike's company. Then, in December, he disappeared again. I tried to get him to come back but was

unsuccessful. I never heard from him again. I tried to call and text a few more times, but when I didn't get a response, I gave up. Sammy did not share any information with me. I couldn't bear to go back to the meetings without Mike, so I gave up on them too.

Back at home, we did not know what was happening, but two phone calls were about to change our world. The first call came on a Thursday evening in early January. I called Mike on my way to Bible study. I didn't expect him to pick up and had planned to leave a message, but to my surprise he picked up after a couple rings.

"Hey, Mikey. Sup, dawg?"

"Yo, yo, Mommadukes, good to hear from you."

"Hey, what are your plans for tonight?"

"Ha-ha, funny you should ask. I'm on my way to Denver."

"What are you going to do in Denver?"

"Me and three guys are on our way to buy drugs."

"Yeah, right, you're so full of it!" I said as my stomach lurched.

"No, Mom, that's exactly what I am doing! I'm driving in a blizzard with three of my friends to get drugs. Gotta go now, we're there, I'll call you later." *Click.*

I was dumbfounded. I tried to call him back, but his phone rolled over to his voice mail. I left a message: "I'm praying for you. Call me when you get back to Carbondale."

I was terrified for Mike. I tried to stay calm as I drove. While I was at Bible study Mike texted me several times to inform me of his progress driving home. I was so panicked inside while this was happening that I barely paid attention to what was being said and had a hard time sitting still.

At the end of Bible study, we shared prayer requests. I broke down sobbing and told my friends what was happening. They formed a circle around me, held my hands, and prayed for my peace of mind. They prayed for Mike and his friends' safety. I felt such unconditional love, and there was no judgment in that room.

On the drive home, I was much calmer. I called Allan about this latest event.

Mike texted me around midnight to say that he had made it back safely to Carbondale. He thanked me for calling and for praying for him.

The ghastly details of that evening still send my heart racing and turn my palms sweaty. I had thought Mike was clean and sober. This conversation took me by complete surprise. I felt Mike had let me down once more. I was scared for him and his friends. I didn't know if I could withstand another relapse. I was physically and emotionally tired, and this was another drain on my resources, which were quickly depleting. Mike was so far away from me. My motherly instinct wanted to get him, protect him, and keep him safe. But I could not do that.

After that night, Mike continued using. It didn't take long for his roommates to realize he had relapsed; since his roommates were in recovery, they kicked him out of the apartment. For the first time in his life, he was without a place to live.

The second call was one Mike made to Brenda, asking if he could stay with her again for a few days. He didn't tell her about his using. But the recovery community is a tight-knit group, and Brenda already knew what had happened. She desperately wanted to help Mike and said yes. She believed that if he lived there, she could watch over him and help find him a treatment program. She viewed it as another chance to save him. But it was a chance that quickly overwhelmed her.

Over the course of the next two weeks, Mike turned Brenda's life upside down once more. He used heroin at her place. She drove him to Denver so he could purchase drugs and allowed him to use nonstop while he was there. Mike missed his shifts at work, and Brenda covered for him. His bosses and coworkers were very concerned about his continued absences and asked Brenda what was going on. As she had during his April relapse, she kept her explanations purposefully vague: he needed some time off; he'd been through a lot recently. Brenda later told me that she felt she had contributed to Mike's relapse by allowing her friendship with him to cloud her vision.

The conversations I had with her during that time painted a pretty clear picture of how fast Mike was spiraling downhill. Some days she would arrive home after a long day at work to find him lying on the couch, eyes closed, with the TV remote in hand. Surrounding him were dirty dishes that had not been there when she left in the morning: a bowl of dried spaghetti and a fork stuck to it by the hardened noodles, a paper plate with an old, partially eaten meat sandwich lying on the table. Chinese takeout containers, half empty. A glass of orange juice sitting precariously on a magazine, just waiting for someone to bump the table and spill it. An ice cream container dripping its melted leftovers down the edge of the table to pool on the carpet.

Other days, she came home to find his bedroom door shut and her two dogs lying right in front of it.

Rapping lightly on his door, she'd call, "I'm back. Are you okay?"

"Sure, fine," Mike would respond through the door, barely audible.

This daily situation wore on her. She had a hard time functioning at work, especially when her coworkers got in her face about where Mike was. She was also missing AA meetings, which were core to her sobriety.

One day, after a particularly stressful day, she came home to Mike sitting on the couch, wearing the same clothes from a couple days ago, eyes blurry and unable to focus. She'd had enough.

"Mike. Mike! I have to talk to you."

"No. Leave me alone," he snapped.

"You have to do something about your addiction. I can't handle coming home and seeing you like this! I'm scared I might come home one day and find you dead. Please, let's do something. I'll help you find a treatment center!"

Mike shook his head. "I'm not ready to quit." With that he walked—or, really, staggered—to his room and slammed his door.

The last straw was when she came home from work a few evenings later to find Mike's mattress on the couch and him standing on it, broom in hand, pounding the ceiling overhead. He claimed that the upstairs neighbors were being too loud and had disturbed him. Brenda didn't know them well at all, and she was very angry with Mikey. She asked Jordan and their mutual friend, Tom, to come over and talk to Mike. When they arrived, Mike didn't want to talk to either of them. After a little coaxing, Mike said he would talk only to Jordan, and after that he settled down a bit.

Distraught, Brenda sat down at her computer and began to google inpatient centers from coast to coast. She called each for admission requirements and information on insurance coverage. Many of the centers had no immediate openings; some did not have detox units, which Mike needed. The centers that had both wouldn't be covered by Mike's insurance.

Brenda babysat Mike for a few more days, trying to keep him safe while he was using. After work each day, she searched for rehabs for him. This was a no-win situation for both; he continued in his relapse, and she tried to live her life as if this current situation didn't affect her. But, as any loved one of an actively using addict knows, addiction affects every aspect of your life: physical, mental, and emotional.

The only information I had during this time came via phone calls and texts from Brenda. Mike had stopped calling me altogether, I think in part because of the shame he felt about his relapse. He was not mentally or emotionally able to come to terms with his addiction himself.

I felt so helpless, fourteen hundred miles away from my son. I knew intellectually that this situation was out of my control. I needed to let Mike suffer the consequences of his relapse. He and Brenda had to work this out together, and Brenda had to make her own decisions. I would support her in helping Mike, but from this distance all I could do was pray that Mike stayed alive long enough to get back into rehab. This downward spiral had to end.

Still, not being able to be with Mike was heart wrenching. Getting up every day and trying to function was extremely difficult. I was angry with Mike not so much for his using as for what he was putting Brenda through. His good friend only wanted to help him, but he was putting her sobriety and job in jeopardy.

I couldn't call my friends to ask for help. It was mentally exhausting just thinking about having those conversations, and I couldn't bring myself to even pick up the phone. I isolated myself.

Allan was supportive, but he needed to focus on his work, and I hated to burden him with my fears and worries. I didn't want to call Dan or Sean either. They were dealing with their own feelings about Mike's addiction. I didn't think it was fair to unload on them.

Some days I put on my mask of being just fine when I knew I wasn't. I'd force myself through the motions of my day. Sometimes I turned to the comfort of eating junk food, fast food, and my favorite: ice cream.

But that relief was short lived, and then I would plunge into a free fall of anger, anxiety, and worry. In the midst of this I realized I was powerless again. Why didn't I see it before? It goes right back to the first three steps of AA.

I admitted my powerlessness over Mike, his using, and what the next few weeks held for him in Colorado.

I needed to believe that a power greater than myself could restore my sanity. My emotional life was feeling pretty out of control. *This is bigger than me,* I told myself.

I made the decision to let God help me with this struggle.

It's not a magic formula, but as I began to work through each step, I felt the stress and anxiety begin to lift. I had to take it one day at a time, and I had to trust God once more for what I could not control.

I heard relief in Brenda's voice a few days later when she called me with some really great news.

"Linda, I found a treatment center in Florida that has an immediate opening! It's called the Florida Center for Recovery, in Orlando."

"Oh, Brenda! That is wonderful news. When does he leave?"

"He leaves tomorrow afternoon. I'm going to drive him to Aspen, where he'll take a commuter plane to Denver, then catch a flight to Orlando. I've asked Joe and Peter to drive along with us. Just to make sure he gets there."

"Brenda, thank you so much for taking care of Mike and finding a treatment center for him. Let me know what I can do from this end to help you."

"Linda, thanks. I've made the plane reservation already. I will get his suitcase packed tonight. I'll let you know when I drop him off in Aspen, okay?"

"That would be great. Tell him I love him."

"I will. Love you too."

"Love you, B."

Phew! Mike left for Florida the next afternoon. I'm sure it didn't come soon enough for Brenda. Nearly eight years later, she told me about the trip.

> I took him into the Aspen airport and waited while he checked in. As Mike put his bag on the counter to have it checked, a bag of gummy bears fell out of his jacket pocket.
>
> He'd told me before we left that he'd glued a package of heroin to the inside of the gummy bears. When I told him that wasn't a good idea, he shrugged it off and stated that he needed a fix or two before he entered treatment.
>
> He grabbed the gummies and stuffed them back into his pocket. Then he quickly turned away from the counter and bolted over to me. I walked with him as far as the TSA checkpoint. I waited to make sure he'd make it through the checkpoint. The TSA agent randomly pulled him aside and did a gun residue check, which Mike passed. He'd cruised by, once again. He turned and waved to me with an impish grin.
>
> When I returned to the car, Joe asked, "What took so long?" I explained what happened, and he wondered what would have happened if TSA had found the heroin. I replied that Mike would be going to jail instead of treatment. We just shook our heads as we headed back to Carbondale.

I called Mike after he arrived in Denver and before his flight to Orlando. He was remorseful for what he'd put Brenda through and what he was putting his family through. I could hear in his voice his disappointment with himself. He talked about the overwhelming guilt and intense shame he was feeling with this relapse. He said he was willing to try another treatment center. Still, I was concerned he would try to leave the airport in order to use.

Was Mike ready for treatment, or was I hearing a heroin addict coming down from his latest high? I pushed that negative thought out of my mind. I wanted to be positive for Mike's sake, yet, at the same time, I did not want to be disappointed again.

It was a huge relief to me when he called to let me know he had landed in Orlando. He told me a representative from the center had met him at the gate and was escorting him from the airport to the recovery center. Once he arrived, he would fill out the paperwork and enter detox. It seemed like things were falling into place, but only time would tell.

We didn't hear anything from him for several days. Then we received a phone call from his counselor telling us that Mike wanted to leave. We had a conference call with Mike and his counselor. Mike told us he wanted to leave. He didn't like it there. They didn't treat him right. It was too restrictive with all their rules.

I understood what he meant. These were code words for "I want to use." I encouraged him to stay in the treatment center. To give it some more time. Mike wasn't sure what he was going to do. He hung up the phone.

Four days later I received a call from the center.

"Hello, Linda. This is Mike's counselor. I am wondering, when did you talk to Mike last?"

"I haven't talked to him since our conference call. Why?"

"Well, he left the center yesterday. I thought you ought to know."

"Ugh! Do you know where he went? Did someone pick him up?"

"All I know is he packed his things and checked himself out."

"Oh! This is just so disappointing." My heart sunk with sadness.

"I understand how frustrating this is for you." She sounded genuinely sorry. "I wish I had more information for you."

"Yeah, me too. If you hear anything from him, please let me know."

"Of course, I will call you if I do. And if you hear anything from Mike, give me a call."

"I will. And thank you for letting me know."

After we hung up, I laid my head on the counter and cried.

"Oh, God, not again. I just can't believe this is happening," I said out loud to the empty kitchen.

I took a few slow deep breaths in and out. I walked around the kitchen reciting the Serenity Prayer and then said a quick prayer for Mike, wherever he was. Then I grabbed my phone and punched in Allan's work number. When he answered, I spewed out my conversation with the counselor. Allan gently reminded me that we couldn't do much from Minnesota and we'd just have to wait to hear from Mike. Logically I knew that, but my mother's heart told me something different.

It didn't take me long after that to panic. I called Mike and texted him. No response. I hit redial again and again. I sent text after text. I paced throughout the house as I waited.

A couple hours later, Mike finally called me. And I went ballistic on him.

"Where are you, and what are you doing?!" I screamed into the phone. "I cannot believe you left there! You need to get back into treatment NOW!" Every fiber in my body was on fire with panic.

"I just didn't like it there, so I left." His response was indifference.

"I'm not stupid, you little shit! You left because you wanted to use."

He didn't answer that accusation, knowing it was true.

I needed to calm down. I told myself to breathe: *Inhale one, two, three... exhale one, two, three...* I took in a deep breath. I exhaled again as I walked out to the front porch and sat on the swing. The fresh air and the swinging motion helped calm me down. Those few seconds gave me the time I needed to gain some perspective and talk rationally to him.

"So, what's your game plan?" I asked.

"I don't have one right now. I know I need to go back to Colorado. I know if I stay here in Florida, I will continue down this dark road."

"That's true, Mike. But I am so worried about you being there. You're out there by yourself; you don't have any friends, no money. I mean, really, you need to figure something out."

"I know that, Mom! I just need to think clearly, which I'm not doing right now."

"Mike, please, be careful out there. God knows what could happen to you in your current state of mind."

"Mom, I will be careful. I gotta go. I will call you once I have a plan. Okay?"

"Okay, Mike. I love you. Take care, and *please* keep in touch!"

"I promise. And I love you too."

I didn't hear any more from him that day, but I texted him that evening and the next day. I feared for him. I knew it was out of my hands and I needed to trust God with my son, but right then, trusting Him was really hard to do.

The scenario would be terrifying for any parent. Mike was in Florida, a place he'd never been before. He was fresh out of detox and clearly craving heroin. He was alone; he had no friends there and no place to stay. I imagined him doing unthinkable things to get drugs: selling his body for cash, stealing money, dealing again, and buying drugs that were laced with God knows what. Yet what could I do for my son when he was so far away? I felt so helpless. I cried out to God to keep Mike safe.

The next day, I received an instant message from Angie, one of Mike's closest friends in the Twin Cities, asking me to give her a call. I immediately punched in her number.

"Hey, Ang. What's going on?"

"Mike texted me. He's in Denver in a motel room, and he's using!"

"In Denver. Really! He's been in Orlando. Did you know that?"

"No, I didn't! I called him after he texted. He said he didn't know what to do next. I didn't know what that meant. He really sounds like he's in a bad place. I am really scared for him."

"Oh, I am so glad you reached out to me. I just don't know what to think or do myself. This has been a long couple of weeks with him in and out of treatment, leaving the state, and now back in Denver and using. I'm so confused and worried. I just don't know what will happen next."

"I knew I needed to get ahold of you, and when you didn't pick up your phone, I sent that message."

"Did he say anything else? Who he was with, what he was using, anything?"

"No, just that he was just in Denver using."

"I hope he gets in touch with me soon. He told me he would, but I haven't heard from him."

"That's got to be so scary for you."

"It is. I just wish he was back here where I could help him."

"I'm sure you do, Linda. Let me know if you hear from him, okay?"

"I will. You do the same, all right?"

"You know I will."

"Yes, I do. Thanks, Angie." As I disconnected, I couldn't help but wonder what would happen next.

Then, almost instantaneously, Mike texted me. I called him, and he picked up.

"I am so worried about you, Mike. What's going on?" My anxiety level rose further.

"I know; that's why I texted you. I'm okay, not great, but hanging in there." I detected disappointment in his voice.

"Are you ready to go back to treatment?"

"No, I'm not. Let's talk about something else. Okay?"

I stared at the phone in my hand. I didn't understand

why he was so reluctant to return to treatment when he knew he needed it.

He told me about his trip to Florida and the treatment center. He never did tell me how he got back to Denver. In the midst of our conversation, I forgot to ask him. To this day it is still a mystery.

We talked for more than half an hour. Mike admitted to feeling tremendous guilt and overwhelming shame about his relapse. He poured his heart out to me; I listened.

He and I had this connection like soulmates. I spoke his language. I related to him in ways Allan, Dan, and Sean couldn't, and he felt free to call me when he felt most vulnerable. I told Mike that I needed to know he was okay, to keep in touch. He promised he would. What I was pleading for was confirmation that he was still alive. I think he understood that.

Allan offered to talk to Mike before he hung up, but Mike said no. I think Mike felt unable to share with his dad that he had once again messed up; all Mike's shame was screaming what a fuck-up he was. I told Mike that his dad loved him and would be there for him. Mike said he'd call Sammy too. Mike told me that he knew he needed a treatment facility that had lockdown and would take his plastic and cash. That was a good sign, but it was Friday afternoon—a bad time to start coordinating between his insurance and a treatment center. He said he was not sure he was ready for it.

After we hung up, I sobbed. Allan held me close as all my emotions and fears rocked me. I felt so drained. How much longer could I continue this roller-coaster ride without a breakdown myself? I just didn't know. At least for the time being I knew he was alive. That was enough for me.

That evening, in the midst of all that turmoil with Mike, Allan and I attended a memorial birthday celebration for Cooper, the son of our friends Kristine and Alex, who had died at age twelve from an undiagnosed heart condition. At the end of the evening, when the hall was just about empty, a mutual friend of ours asked to pray for Mike.

We huddled together with Pastor Nate and Miriam in the middle of the room and prayed for about ten minutes. Less than ten seconds after we'd said amen, Allan's cell phone rang. He answered and mouthed to me, "It's Dan. He's crying."

Allan walked to the other side of the room while he talked to Dan. I stood with our friends, making small talk, but anxiously waiting to hear what Dan had called about. When they hung up, Allan returned to our group.

"You aren't going to believe this! Dan just got off the phone with Mike. He spent the past hour talking to him. Mike is good, and he's starting to think seriously about treatment."

All of us let out a shout of "Hallelujah!"

"Mike isn't bingeing," Allan continued. "In fact, Dan couldn't even tell he was using. He said his speech was clear and normal. He and Mike shared some childhood stories, and Dan feels really good about where Mike is at mentally. Mike said he'd keep in touch with Dan over the weekend.

Dan cried the entire time he talked with me, and Dan is not a crier."

All of us had tears running down our cheeks by this time. That phone call precisely at that time was exactly what we needed to hear; it was God calling in to answer our prayers. When we left the celebration for Cooper, it felt like it had also been a celebration for what God was doing in Mikey's current situation.

Later that night, Sean called to talk to me about the evening's events. He cried for his little brother. Like Dan, Sean is not someone who cries easily. And, also like Dan, Sean's heart was breaking and there was nothing he could do for his little brother. We all slept better that night knowing Mike was safe—and God was in charge. Mike texted me a few times that night and again Saturday morning to tell me he was doing okay and he loved me. Mike kept his promise to Dan and texted him too.

One of the real ironies of this whole ordeal is that Mike felt so alone. He told me so several times in our discussions. But, in fact, he had family members and many close friends around the country reaching out to him. I don't just mean people praying for him—that is very important—but also people who called him, texted him, and mailed him encouraging notes, from his friends and recovering addicts in Colorado to his former counselor in Denver, the mom of his ex-roommate, and his friends here in Minnesota. A customer from City Market left him a Valentine's Day card at the store. I received phone calls out of the blue from friends, friends' mothers, and many others with encouraging words for Mikey. None of us were alone.

On Sunday, February 19, I received some good news. Darlene, the mother of Mike's friend Troy, called me from Denver to say that Mike was safe in detox at PVH. Whew!

Monday night brought better news. Mike called us from detox. He was clearly struggling with what had happened, but for the first time in three weeks he was thinking clearly and logically. He was remorseful, contrite, and very apologetic about what had happened. (If you're counting, this was his sixth time in treatment.) He referenced the hell he knew he'd put all of us through but expressed optimism for his future.

He hated what had happened in Florida. He couldn't explain it; only that he couldn't overcome his defiance at the Florida center and had to leave. He was grateful to be back at PVH.

Mike explained to us that his counselor, Matt, had told him he needed to begin thinking about long-term psychiatric counseling after treatment or he would continue relapsing every nine to twelve months, as was his habit. Allan told Mike he'd mentioned that to me recently as well. Mike made reference to his long talk with Dan on Friday night, too: that talk with his big brother had a real impact, and somehow that had turned his thinking around. Allan and I were cheered by Mike's enthusiasm to get clean and stay that way, but this was not the first time we'd heard him talk like that; I'd say we were cautiously optimistic. We had already been on this roller-coaster ride too many times to take Mike at his word. We needed to see some follow-through from him.

Meanwhile, in the past few weeks my dad had started

physically going downhill. Allan, Sean, and I planned to drive to Wisconsin on Tuesday morning to visit him and my stepmom. At around 6:30 a.m., my stepmom called to say that my dad had passed away a couple hours earlier. I had been preparing myself for his death since his health had begun deteriorating and he had entered hospice at home several months earlier. Still, it was really hard to lose my dad. We had developed a closer relationship since Mike's addiction began.

I woke up Allan as soon as I'd hung up the phone and then called Dan and Sean to let them know about Grampa Red. Instead of driving to Wisconsin that day as planned, we would wait until funeral arrangements had been made.

Mike was unaware of my dad's recent decline and, now, his death. I called Sammy to ask his opinion on when to tell Mike. He suggested that we wait to tell Mike until he was out of detox, so he could concentrate on that. When we broke the news later that week, Mike took it in stride, although I don't think his mind was completely processing information yet in the wake of his relapse. He would not be able to attend the funeral—another important family event missed due to his addiction.

My dad's funeral was held on Saturday, February 25, and our family gathered for a sad but welcome reunion. My sister Candee and her husband, Michael, flew in Tuesday evening from Massachusetts. I made the three-hour drive the next day. My dad's younger brother Jim, my cousin Amy, and her husband Cain drove in from Indiana on Friday, as did my aunt Harriet and my sister Tracy and her family. Allan, Dan, and Sean drove over Saturday morning. It was good to be surrounded by family as we laid my dad to rest in a wonderful tribute to a life well lived.

I had a very hard time accepting the fact that Mike couldn't be there. I don't think my family members were as acutely aware of it as I was. Though I know much about addiction and its effects on the family structure, when it came to my own son missing his grandfather's funeral, the grief grew even more painful. I was grieving the loss of my dad and, at the same time, grieving for my addicted son.

16. A Deep Pit

Mike's planned release date was Sunday, March 18. Things went fairly smoothly until the week before, when he called us early Saturday morning with a bombshell: he planned to leave PVH early and move in with his girlfriend, Rebecca, sharing a one-bedroom apartment.

Mike had met Rebecca in treatment. She was a recovering alcoholic just one month into her sobriety. No treatment facility would ever recommend establishing a romantic relationship during your first months of recovery, especially with another addict or alcoholic, and surely not moving in together. Unfortunately, there wasn't a lot we could do to intervene in his plans.

On Sunday night I texted Mike and asked him to call me when he had time—I wanted to discuss those plans. He never responded to that text. Things went south very quickly after that.

Tuesday night, Mike left PVH against medical advice and used. He called his counselor, Matt, to tell him he was at a motel and speedballing: using heroin with cocaine, morphine, or an amphetamine, usually via injection—an extremely dangerous combination.[15]

Matt called the sheriff to do a welfare check on Mike; the sheriff took him to the hospital. Mike was released on Wednesday and went back to PVH, but on Thursday night he called friends, who picked him up at PVH. They went out and bought drugs, then dropped off Mike at a motel, where he planned to use and meet Rebecca. However, when Mike called Rebecca to tell her his plan, she was so concerned that she called the sheriff's office. They sent an officer to conduct another welfare check, and Mike was again taken by ambulance to the local hospital, where he spent the night and was released the next day. Rebecca took him back to PVH on Friday.

Allan talked to Mike on Friday afternoon. Mike was really feeling down. His dad asked him if it would be a good idea for one of us to come visit him at PVH. Mike immediately said yes. Allan talked to Matt, who was very enthusiastic about the idea. Then we talked to Mikey again that night. I asked him which of us he wanted to come out, and he said his dad. Allan quickly began making plans for his trip. He reserved a rental car and began packing, planning to leave Saturday night, which was St. Patrick's Day.

In the middle of Friday night, I received a call from PVH. Mike had left and used, and they had found suicide notes in the trash can in his room.

I felt shaken to my core. I had never even considered that Mike would seriously contemplate taking his own life. Throughout his battle, Mike had never indicated that he wanted to end his life except that once, early in his addiction, when I believe he meant it as a call for help. He had lived his life in the fast lane and seemed to enjoy it; this was a complete turnaround. I think the buildup of shame over the past several weeks of relapse had affected Mike in a new way. He was no longer working out and taking care of his body. I think his thoughts were clouded by his drug use. Mike had told me several months earlier that each relapse dug him into a deep pit and each time it was harder to find his way out and stay out.

The staff of PVH told me the sheriff had been called to find him. Several hours later, the sheriff found Mike, who was having a medical emergency. The sheriff believed it was an attempted suicide by overdose and took him to the emergency room. I immediately called the ER and talked to the nurse on duty.

She told me that Mike was there and was very despondent, but she couldn't share anything more. Mike had refused to sign an authorization form giving them permission to share information with us. It was another sleepless night as I waited to hear from Mike.

On Saturday morning Allan called the ER and talked to the nurse on duty for the day, who gave him a little more information about Mike's condition. Mike's vital signs were good; he was mentally and physically exhausted, and the ER doctor was deciding what Mike needed next.

Mike would not talk to either of us at this point. I think his continued use and his physical and mental deterioration, along with the overwhelming shame he felt after this relapse, kept him from reaching out to us.

My day was fraught with anxiety as I waited to talk to him before his dad left. After we made several attempts to reach Mike, he finally called us. Allan and I were both on the phone with him when he broke down sobbing.

"I don't know what to do. I don't know what to do," Mike repeated over and over. "I'm so scared I'll hurt myself."

"Mike, we're here for you," I said to him tenderly. "While you're in the ER, they will help keep you safe. So please don't try to leave again, okay?"

"I won't, Mom. When is Dad coming out?"

"I'm leaving this evening," Allan answered. "I plan on driving straight through to get there. Okay?"

"Please hurry, Dad. I really need you. I feel so lost."

"I will, Mike. You hang in there, buddy. I love you."

"I love you both. Bye."

Allan and I were both pretty shaken up about Mike's emotional condition. I hoped that Allan's arrival in Colorado would boost Mike's spirits. He left around 9:00 p.m. and drove all night, sleeping at a rest stop for about four hours somewhere in the middle of Nebraska. He arrived in Denver on Sunday afternoon. After he checked into his motel, he went to see Mike. He got terribly lost on the way to the hospital but finally found it. Mike was meeting with a social worker in the locked-down psychiatric unit when Allan arrived, but when Mike saw his dad, he ran out of the office. He hugged Allan tightly and cried like a baby. Then Allan joined him in the meeting and other medical appointments. Afterward, they talked about this latest relapse. Allan could tell it had taken its toll on Mike. His son looked different: he had lost weight and looked haggard, and his eyes had lost their glimmer.

That evening Rebecca dropped by for a visit with Mike

and Allan finally got to meet her. The three of them talked for a while, and then Allan headed to the motel because he was exhausted from his long trip.

On Monday Allan visited Mike and met with Matt. Allan thought the counselor was a good man. Sammy called Allan and offered to meet with him and Mike as well. Allan hesitated at first, but it turned out to be a good idea. When Sammy arrived at the hospital, Mike ran into his arms and gave him one of his big, heartfelt hugs. The three of them talked about old times, Allan's drive out, and, of course, what was next for Mike. It was a good visit. Rebecca joined them later on and met Sammy for the first time. The three of them hung out with Mike for a while longer, and then Sammy and Allan went out to dinner.

On Tuesday Allan met with Mike and his social worker to develop a plan: intensive outpatient (IOP) treatment at West Pines in Denver and long-term psychiatric counseling. Mike made arrangements to stay with his friend Troy's parents during his IOP. That was a major breakthrough because Mike needed to line up a place to stay before he was discharged from the hospital. That was another answer to our prayers.

On Wednesday Allan reserved a U-Haul truck in Carbondale to pick up the belongings Mike would need during IOP. That evening, Allan, Sammy, Rebecca, and another friend of Mike's came for a short visit. After Rebecca left, Mike proposed an idea to his dad: he wanted to drive home with Allan and make amends to his brothers and me. Allan thought this was a good idea. Sammy thought so too. So Allan and Mike began making plans for the trip home.

Mike was discharged the afternoon of Thursday, March 22, with plans in place for his IOP and counseling to begin after he returned from Minnesota. Mike called me after he'd been discharged, but he didn't tell me he was coming home. They spent the night at a motel, and the next day they went to Brenda's to pick up Mike's car. It was a bittersweet stop for Mike and Brenda. They had been through a lot together, especially during the past eight weeks. It was hard for Brenda to say goodbye to Mike even though she knew he was doing the right thing.

Mike and Allan headed to Carbondale, Allan in the rental car and Mike in his car. They stopped at Subway for lunch. As they found a table, a woman with a guide dog had a seizure and fell to the floor near the counter. Mike jumped up to assist her as his EMT training kicked in. He squatted down to stabilize her so she wouldn't hurt herself and waited for the seizure to end. Even though he was in a bad place himself, he was deeply compassionate and never let his struggles stand in the way of helping others. To Mike this was no big deal; no matter what your own circumstances are, you can always help someone else.

After lunch, they picked up the U-Haul in Carbondale, returned the Denver rental car, and packed up Mike's belongings from his apartment. Then they headed back to Denver again, Mike in his car and Allan driving the truck. It was a long day and emotionally draining for both of them. They went out to dinner and then returned to the motel. Allan told me about an unforgettable exchange he had there with Mike:

I went to wash my hands, and there was no soap in our room. The motel maid didn't leave any when she cleaned our room. I called the front desk and complained in what I thought was a polite manner. I walked down to get the soap at the front desk, and when I returned Mike gently noted that I shouldn't have been so rude to the woman at the front desk. She wasn't the one who forgot to give us soap. I defended myself feebly, and that was the end of our discussion. We were both very tired.

I slept on our discussion and Mike's gentle rebuke of my behavior. The next morning, I got up before Mike to take a note to the front desk apologizing for my curt words the night before. To my surprise, the same woman was still working, so I apologized in person, explaining to her that my son had overheard me talking to her last night and told me I was rude. While driving back to Minnesota later that day, I felt so proud and righteous for how I had apologized, so I told Mike. He didn't say a word. You see, in his mind, I should have never spoken that way to begin with and my apology was the very least I could do to make up for my poor behavior. I suspect that in Mike's mind, my apology didn't deserve any special recognition. And, of course, he was right.

That afternoon, they rented a storage unit and unloaded Mike's stuff into it. They dropped off Mike's car at Sammy's house and said their goodbyes to him, and then they jumped in the rental car and began their trip home to Minnesota.

They stopped before dusk at the Blue River Rest Area near Seward, Nebraska, just west of Lincoln. Allan and

Mike walked down a path and over a bridge that crossed the Blue River, which Mike noted was more green than blue because of the algae. Allan took Mike's picture in the parking lot as the sun was setting, its rays reflecting off the back of a semitruck parked there. Mike's face reflected his tiredness but mostly the sadness in his eyes. We would use this photo for Mike's prayer card at his funeral. Mike was subdued most of the ride home and slept a lot.

At around 11:00 p.m. they stopped in Des Moines, Iowa, where they had planned on staying overnight. When they realized that they could be home in three and a half hours, however, they decided to press on.

Allan told me later that Mike was planning to buy me a bouquet of flowers. They stopped just south of Saint Paul at around 2:00 a.m., hoping that the local grocery store would be open. It wasn't, so they arrived home at 2:30 a.m. on Sunday morning, March 25, without flowers but bringing me something so much more important: my son.

I heard noises downstairs and got up to investigate. Allan startled me on the steps—he wasn't supposed to be home for hours yet! He told me to wait for him in the kitchen. As I stepped into the kitchen, Mike walked in the back door. I was so surprised to see him. I hugged and kissed him, crying the whole time. It was so good to see him in the flesh. He was very pleased with himself for pulling off the surprise. We chatted briefly before going to bed. It took me a long time to fall asleep. I was elated to have Mike home.

17. Mike's Homecoming

Mike's initial plan was to stay until Tuesday or Wednesday and then fly back to Denver and begin his IOP. On Sunday evening a good friend of Mike's from AA in Colorado, Wickes, called. He was in Minnesota to attend a relative's wedding. He had no idea that Mike was in town; he had just called to say that he was in Mike's home state. Mike was very excited to talk to his friend. As it turned out, Wickes would be in Minnesota until April 4 and would then be driving back to Carbondale. This got Mike to thinking about staying longer at home, and he proposed driving back with Wickes as far as Denver. His friend was eager to have Mike's company on the long trip back. Then Mike discussed his idea with his dad and me, and we agreed he could stay. That unexpected phone call turned out to be a blessing for our family, as Mike spent eleven days at home with us.

Mike jumped into the visit with gusto. He got together with many friends he hadn't seen since his move in 2010. Mike was coming and going all the time, keeping late-night hours and often sleeping until noon. His cell phone was always pinging with text messages or calls from his friends.

He needed to stay busy: sitting around doing nothing was hazardous to Mike's well-being.

During the first few days he was home, I had a lot of anxiety and didn't sleep well. I was concerned about Mike staying here for that long and worried about the possibility of a relapse. But that was something I could not control. I talked to Mike about my feelings, and he understood them. He explained to me that he knew what he was doing. There were things he wanted to do and people he wanted to connect with while he was home. He couldn't alleviate my fears; that was my responsibility. He wanted me to understand that.

Now the shoe was on the other foot: he was helping me to see that perhaps I was the one beginning to relapse. I could not control what might happen in Mike's life while he was home. I could only control what was happening in my own life.

I needed to work my own Al-Anon program to keep my sanity. I had let my worry for Mike lead me away from what I knew I needed to do for me. I had been attending Al-Anon frequently over the past few months, but I had stopped going to meetings and doing my self-care while Mike was home. I recommitted to attending a daily meeting while Mike was home. It was hard to walk into that first meeting and share what had been going on in my life recently, but once I got rolling and saw the nods and smiles from the others, I relaxed and felt like I'd come back home. After that meeting I made myself a priority by continuing to go to meetings, reading my daily meditations, and doing things with my friends. I tried to maintain my normal schedule by getting up each day at my normal time, working out, doing household chores, running errands, and so on. I needed to do these things to keep the feeling of insanity at bay. After those initial few days, I began to relax and really enjoy having Mike home.

Mike worked his program, too, by attending several AA/NA meetings. He kept us informed of his plans. When he went out, he told us who he was with and where he'd be. I think he wanted to help alleviate some of my anxiety. He didn't say that, but his actions did, and I really appreciated it. When he was home, we hung out together. He and I talked about many things, especially his addiction and relapses, and his fears about going back to Colorado and resuming his life after IOP. Some evenings when he was home, he came into the family room to talk while I was watching TV. Before I knew it, he'd finagled one of the backrubs that he so loved and I so enjoyed giving.

Mike also spent time with his two brothers. They golfed, went out to dinner, and just hung out. I dropped off Mike at Dan's house for a couple nights, and he ended up helping Dan with a couple home projects.

Before I knew it, the eleven days were coming to an end. On his last night home, the five of us had a barbecue at our house. There was a lot of laughter and good-natured banter among all of us, just like it was before heroin. After dinner, Mike, Dan, and Sean stood in the backyard together, having a smoke. I was out of earshot, but I could see them talking and laughing together. It was good to see that. They needed that time, just the three of them. We called it an early evening because Mike would be getting up early to leave the next morning.

Wickes arrived at our house at 5:00 a.m. Before long they were on the road to Colorado. Mike called us that evening to let us know Wickes had dropped him off in Denver and he was at Stan and Darlene's house, where he would be staying during his IOP.

Mike settled in and began his IOP at West Pines, a short distance away. Stan and Darlene were another real blessing for Mike. He felt comfortable with them, and their home was a good and safe place to stay.

I hadn't met Darlene, another of Mike's Colorado moms, at this point. She and I had talked on the phone and texted several times. We shared the joys and sorrows of having chemically dependent sons. She once texted me, "There is something very mysterious about the souls of addicts that I would love to discover. It's hard to explain, but there is something very loving and caring about them. BIG mystery—they have so much to offer; for me it's kind of like being around young children and babies—I just want to squeeze them."

I would agree.

Mike and Darlene had spent time together after Mike's IOP and while her husband was out of town for business. Mike was a big fan of the Minnesota Wild hockey team, and Darlene watched the games with him.

One evening, as the game began before Mike got out to watch, Darlene hollered to him, trying to match his slang, "Move it, bread slice!"

Mike walked into the room, laughing his butt off. "Momma D, it's home slice."

(I'd have been right there with Darlene, I admit. I looked that phrase up in the Advanced English Dictionary: it means a fellow or a male acquaintance from one's hometown.)

Allan and I received a call a few days later to tell us that Mike had ended up in the ER on April 18 after another relapse. The next day he was discharged to West Pines inpatient treatment for three weeks. He moved in with Sammy until he overdosed again and took another trip to the ER.

After that, I received a call from Mike.

"Hi, Mom," he said quietly.

"Hey, bud, what's up?" I said, fearing what his next statement was going to be.

"I had to move out of Sammy's house because I used there. He said I couldn't stay there anymore; he didn't want me living there because of the risk I pose to his family."

Trepidation filled my heart; my hand shook holding the phone to my ear as I listened. I felt so helpless.

"Mike, I just don't know what to say or do for you."

"You don't have to say or do anything, Mom. This is my problem. You've helped me so much already."

"I suppose you don't know what you're going to do now?"

"No, not right yet, I need to talk to my social worker and doctor. I'll let you know what I'm going to do as soon as I know, okay?"

"Yeah. Okay."

"Bye, Mom. I love you."

"Bye. I love you so much too. Be careful."

"I will."

I was once again hanging on for dear life as the roller coaster plunged down another hill, around a harrowing corner. My heart pounded as I tried to reel in my fear, realizing I was once again speeding along the tracks with no end in sight.

I talked with Mike several times over the next few days. He was broken; once again, he was at a loss.

He would sob over the phone, crying out, "I don't know what to do. I need help. Help me."

Mike went back to West Pines for a few days. I talked with him, his doctor, and his social worker while he was there. We all were in agreement: Mike needed a long-term solution. I looked online for treatment centers that had extended stays. He needed to be at a center for a year or longer.

These centers are very expensive. By this time Mike had used up his college money, and Allan and I weren't in a position to fund a stay like that. Darlene called to tell me she'd heard of a place in Europe that offered treatment at no cost for as long as necessary; you just needed to get him there. I looked into that place, but I didn't want Mike that far away. It was gut wrenching for me. I decided I needed to fly out to my son and help him as best I could. But before I could get my flight booked, Mike called. He and Sammy had decided it would be best if they drove to Minnesota and Mike stayed here while he figured out his next step.

On a sunny Wednesday morning, Mike and Sammy set out in Mike's car for Minnesota. This would be Mike's last road trip with Sammy—or anyone.

They arrived around 10:00 p.m. on Friday evening. Over

the weekend, we made omelets and pancakes for breakfast and steak and burgers for dinner. Mike took Sammy sightseeing around the Twin Cities. On Monday morning all six of us golfed at a local par 3. It was like old times for us, plus Sammy. We laughed and joked at our golf skills as we enjoyed our time together. Sammy flew home that afternoon.

Mike made arrangements to enter Hazelden once again, his eighth and final treatment center stay. On Tuesday, May 22, Allan and I drove Mike there. However, Blue Cross Blue Shield wouldn't cover opiate detox for Mike. We were desperate to get Mike into treatment again. I felt the medical care community was letting us down.

Sammy suggested that Mike get drunk so he would qualify for detox. We stopped on the way so Mike could buy a pint of Jim Beam. Mike did not like to drink alcohol and never had, so it was especially weird as Allan and I watched Mike down several glasses of Jim Beam and Coke. Mike sat in the front seat as Allan drove, and I sat in the back, watching Mike getting drunk. I am not a drinker either, and this situation was utterly surreal. Mike offered me a swig of the Jim Beam, which he knew I'd decline. Allan shook his head no to Mike's offer as well. I didn't like taking this extreme measure to get Mike back into Hazelden, but at this point we were willing to do anything to get Mike into detox.

We drove up to the front door of Hazelden and helped Mike bring his belongings inside. We said our goodbyes to him one more time. I cried as I walked back to the car. The first time we'd brought him here, I'd had confidence that he would come out clean and sober. But after the last four years of addiction and relapses, I felt unsure about how this would be for him. I was cautiously optimistic this time.

Back at home, I went into Mike's room to tidy it up. As I was pulling the bedcovers over his pillow, I noticed blood on his pillowcase. Then I remembered seeing Mike take out his trash, which was unusual for him. I ran outside to the garbage can and looked for the bag he had taken out. I opened the bag. Sure enough, inside were four syringes, one for each day Mike had been home. He'd been using while at home. Combining heroin and alcohol could have been lethal for Mike.

I was sad Mike had been using. I knew enough about addiction to know that this is a common occurrence, but I was disappointed in Mike. When he called a few days later, I confronted him on what I had found. He told me that he couldn't apologize for it; that's just what addicts do—use one last time before going into treatment.

I started referring to his time there as "Camp Hazelden," just a bit of weird humor to keep me sane. Allan and I drove out each Sunday to visit him. Grandma Betty and Aunt Harriet visited him once as well. After Mike's death, they both commented on how glad they were to have gone to see him because that was the last time they saw Mike alive.

Once again, Mike seemed to do really well in the structured treatment setting. He called and told us how good and right it felt for him to be there again. He, of course, fit right in with the other patients, as he always felt he did, due in part to his wit, charm, and easygoing manner. He was free from using and felt physically safe there. He made many friends during his stay, as we came to find out afterward.

This time, his counselor was named Melanie, and he was smitten with her. She was young and attractive, and Mike seemed to enjoy his interactions with her during group and individual sessions. A couple of weeks into Mike's treatment, Melanie asked each of the four of us to write Mike a letter of impact about the effects of his addiction on us.

On Saturday, June 2, Dan, Sean, Allan, and I drove up to meet with Mike and Melanie. It was a very emotional time as we each, in our own way, told Mike about how his addiction had affected us over the past four years of his using. We described how it made us feel, how it affected our family and our relationships with him. We talked about how scared we were of losing him and about his ability to beat this addiction.

Dan told Mike, "You are the strongest person I know, and if anyone can beat this, you can. You need to step up to the plate and do what you need to do. And I love you."

Sean's letter told Mike about the first time he found heroin in their bathroom and Mike lied to him, saying he was holding it for a friend. When Sean found out later that the heroin belonged to Mike, he felt betrayed and disappointed because the two of them had always been honest with each other. Sean told Mike he could beat this addiction but he had to do the work and that Sean loved him very much.

Allan read his letter, and I read mine last. I told Mike how I felt that he had taken advantage of my caring and loving nature so many times over the four years, deliberately lying to me to get money for "rent," only to use it for drugs. How I was so hurt that the man I raised had done this to me. I ended by saying that I loved him, supported him, and knew he could beat this addiction.

The five of us cried as we read our heartfelt words and listened to one another's. Mike broke down as we read our letters to him, visibly moved by our experiences. The room filled with so much emotion that it was hard to breathe. Afterward, Mike talked to Melanie for a few minutes before meeting up with us. That evening, Mike told her and his peers that he felt like, after that meeting, "the world had been lifted from my shoulders."

I was not sure what he meant. Had I received those letters, I would have felt very depressed and sad, even though they affirmed how loved I was; it would have been the total opposite of Mike's response. I asked Sean what he thought Mike meant. He explained that he thought Mike had begun to understand what kind of emotional pain he had put our family through during his addiction and his attempted suicides in Colorado. He knew how we worried about him and thought that it would make it easier on us if he weren't around, making that final choice less difficult for him. Allan had a different take on it. He said he thought our letters had reaffirmed that we loved him and supported him and that we had not deserted him. No matter how we interpreted his statement, Mike knew he was loved no matter what and that we would always be here for him.

We spent an hour or so with Mike after reading him our letters. The weather was warm and sunny as we walked around the grounds together; the three brothers laughed and joked with one another. I took that as a good sign. By the time we left, I think we all felt very good about what we had tried to accomplish. Now it was up to Mike to take charge of his life and his recovery.

Allan and I picked Mike up from Hazelden on Tuesday morning, June 19, after his twenty-eight days. When Mike showed up at the front desk for checkout, his good friend Scott accompanied him. Scott and Mikey were both competitive and enjoyed good-natured but intense sporting activities while they were together at Hazelden. We had met some of Scott's family during our weekend visits, and Scott has continued to bless us with his friendship.

We drove home, and the three of us spent a couple hours together. We ate lunch on the back deck. Then Allan and I drove Mike over to Crossroads, the halfway house he was moving into. The manager of the place gave us a tour; we saw Mike's room and met his roommate. Shortly after that, Allan and I went home. We wanted Mike to get acquainted with his new living arrangements. That evening, I texted with him several times, asking him how he liked the place; he said it would take him some time to feel comfortable living there. I told him I loved him and we'd talk tomorrow.

On Wednesday I didn't hear from Mike until late evening. I had texted him earlier that morning to let him know that our good friends Kristine and Alex were coming over for dinner and would he want to stop by to say hi? He texted back that maybe he would. He didn't. After dinner I texted to say that he had missed a good time with our friends. We exchanged more messages in the easy banter he and I often shared. Before I turned in for the evening, I asked if he would want to get together on Thursday to go biking. He said he would call me about it in the morning.

What we didn't know was that Mike hadn't stayed at Crossroads Tuesday night.

Part Three

Part Three
Part Three
Part Three
Part Three
Part Three
Part Three

18. It's Gonna Be Hard Saying Goodbye to You

Life with an addict is like being caught in a tornado. It swoops in, touches down, and leaves destruction in its aftermath. You may have heard the warning siren go off in your head but ignored it as you observed the swirling winds of out-of-control behavior, the crashing sounds of your home and family being torn apart. Mikey's life cracked and splintered before my eyes; the power lines of love and communication snapped, and heartbreak shattered the windows of my life. For a while I sought shelter in my hopes for his recovery as we waited for this storm to end.

The storm did end, and when we ventured out into the eerie calm, it had taken Mike with it. Nothing remained but wreckage. I took in this unbelievable destruction of our formerly comfortable life, one hand clasped over my mouth and the other clutching my chest. My heart raced as I searched frantically for the trinkets of an irreplaceable life: shreds of holiday family gatherings, kid birthday parties, sleepovers, and the smiles and laughter of days when life was safe and carefree. Those days suddenly seemed so far away. I wondered, *What the hell happened here?*

When you come to this point after a journey like ours, you feel dismayed over all those years of hard work you spent building the familiar life that's now gone. How will you rebuild your life and your family's life? How will you or they ever be the same again, now that your sense of safety and security has been destroyed? Your heart breaks at the immense task that lies ahead. You cry buckets of tears; you yell and swear and shake your fist at God just before you fall facedown, sobbing. That's where you stay for a time until you surrender—to life, to choices, and to a power greater than yourself. Then, slowly, almost imperceptibly, the anger, pain, and tears dissipate and you take one shallow, raspy breath, followed by another, as ever so gently you lift your head up to look around. Then you push yourself up to your knees and sit up. Finally, you stand, weak-kneed; once you get your balance you take a tentative step, thinking you're going to fall but catching yourself. You take another step, this one a little less shaky, and another, and then you breathe.

Those unanswered questions and unresolved inner conflicts mixed with the grief as I looked back and processed my last two days of communication with Mike.

What did I do to deserve this? Why didn't I see it coming? Who do I blame? Who could have stopped this? Am I at fault? Is there anything I could have done to save Mike?

The bottom line is NO. Mike chose to use drugs. As a result, his brain was hijacked and he saw no other way out except to use, which led to his eventual suicide. Mike had the tools he needed to stay clean and sober—tools he had used many times but that failed him in the end. If love could have saved Mike, he would have been saved a hundred times over. He was loved by his dad and me, Dan and

Sean, his extended family, and oh so many friends. But in the end, the power of heroin addiction and the inner turmoil he struggled with left him with only one choice. And that was to end his life.

You never know what you are capable of doing in your lifetime. I never expected to bury any of my children, least of all my youngest son. I'd never given any thought to planning a visitation or funeral for one of my kids. I'd planned on them doing that for me; that's the way it's supposed to be.

We didn't have a choice. We had to jump right in headfirst. The four of us planned everything together. It kept us very busy during those first weeks after Mike's death. I believe that was a good thing because it helped us ease into our grief. Grief is never easy, pleasant, or timely. But the distraction helped stave off the inevitable sorrow we would face in the days, weeks, and months to come.

On Saturday morning, two days after Mike died, Dan, Sean, Allan, and I went to the funeral home to see Mike's body. We were shown into the director's office. While we waited for him, we were quiet and pensive and even a little apprehensive. I was anxious to see my Mikey. It had been four days since my last conversation with him.

The funeral director led us into the room where Mike was lying in the casket. As the four of us walked up, we started crying. It was very traumatic to see his lifeless body. The guys hung back a bit, but I walked right up to him and kissed his cheek. It was so cold. I laid my hand over his heart and put my cheek on his chest and sobbed. My heart pounded inside my chest. I wanted to crawl inside the casket with Mike and never leave him. How was I going to live without him? I cupped his face in my hands, kissed his lips, and then stood aside. As each one of my guys walked up to see Mike, they broke down, looking at him, caressing his face, holding his hand, and whispering in his ear. All the while sobbing as our hearts and lives shattered again.

It reminded me of that Friday night when we confronted Mike about his drug use, the five of us on our back deck, my emotionally strong men reduced to brokenhearted tears. But seeing them now, even more broken, was a thousand times harder than that night. My stomach lurched, and my heart and head throbbed as I wept for my son.

Sean and I clung to each other as we cried after his turn with Mike. After an hour or so, each one of us spent one last time with Mike. I went last to say my goodbye. I held his hand, ran my fingers through his hair, and rubbed his cheek, and then I whispered in his ear, "You little shit." I smiled and gave him one last kiss on his lips, and I walked away.

Everything we did in the aftermath was a group decision. We all four had to agree or we chose another option. The most poignant example I remember is the decision on whether or not to cremate Mike's body. Dan, Allan, and I felt that Mike wouldn't care either way. But Sean couldn't imagine cremating his brother's body. So, we agreed against cremation. That's how all the decisions went, big and small.

On Sunday, after church, Dan, Sean, and I went shopping

for the clothes Mike would wear for the viewing and burial. We chose khaki shorts and a blue striped golf shirt. We kept his same hairstyle and left his facial hair as it was when he was alive. We chose the necklace that he was wearing when he died and one of his big bling watches; he had several to choose from. We picked a newer pair of his athletic shoes.

We also selected a recent photo of Mike for the funeral director to use in cosmeticizing and setting Mike's features so that he would look his very best. We dropped off everything at the funeral home on Tuesday morning.

Allan, Dan, and Sean chose thirty pictures of Mike and the songs for the DVD that would play at the visitation and during the funeral. I had come home that Monday evening to find Dan, Sean, and Allan sitting on the floor in the living room, sorting through pictures. They asked if there were others I wanted.

"Whatever you've picked is just fine with me," I said.

On Tuesday afternoon we mounted the pictures to trifold poster boards. We sat in the living room as we went through a lifetime of family pictures, which invoked much laughter and many tears as we reminisced about Mike.

I remember seeing him at the funeral home the afternoon prior to the visitation—how lifelike he looked. I imagined him sleeping and opening his eyes, saying, "Sup, Mommadukes?" I was very pleased that the director had taken such care in the details to make him look just like he did when he was alive.

The visitation was held on the evening of Wednesday, June 27. It was a beautiful day, and the sun shone brightly in a cloudless sky. Family and close friends arrived at three o'clock to spend time with Mikey before the formal visitation began. Dan, Sean, Allan, and I welcomed Allan's parents, Bob and Val; Lori, Allan's sister from Texas, and her daughter, Juliet, from Alaska; my stepmom, Betty; and my sister Tracy and her children. My other sister, Candee, flew in from Boston, and several of Mike's closest friends flew in from Colorado: Sammy, Brenda, Joe, and Jennifer. It was so important for us to have family and friends here to help say goodbye to Mike before others came to see him. It made the grieving a bit easier.

I will never forget the sadness in the group as we viewed Mike's body for the last time. There lay our precious boy. He found peace at last.

Jon, our dear family friend, had volunteered to ferry people back and forth from the airport, and that was almost a full-time job. Steve, a good friend that Mike met at Hazelden in 2010, drove all the way up from Chicago, met with us at the visitation, and drove back that same night. Another friend, from Mike's last stay at Hazelden, drove with his dad ten hours from North Dakota for the visitation and funeral. Another recovering friend of Mike's drove down from Fargo, North Dakota, for the visitation. We were reminded about the mysterious, invisible communication system that seems to instantaneously link recovering addicts to one another.

More than four hundred people came to visit Mikey that evening. It was a real tribute to the impact Mike had on this world. The line snaked through the funeral home, down the front steps, and around the corner past the parking lot. Eventually the director opened the funeral home's other rooms so people could wait out of the hot, humid weather. The four of us talked briefly to each person who came to see Mikey. I know that slowed things down a bit, but we wanted to make sure we thanked people for coming and supporting us. I remember looking at the door at the back of the room and seeing throngs of people waiting for us and feeling humbled and grateful for each one of them. It was well after 9:00 p.m. before the last person left. It was a long, tiring, and very sad day.

Two details vividly stand out for me from the visitation. The first was seeing Jon sitting in front of Mike's casket, sobbing. He was inconsolable. I tried talking to him, hoping to give him some comfort, but it didn't help at the time.

When I saw Jon again a few weeks later, I asked him about the funeral. He told me that a few winters before, he and Mike had gone ice fishing. Due to a medical issue, Jon had a seizure on the ice. Mike jumped into action, running to get Jon's truck, getting him in it, and taking him to the hospital. Mike literally saved Jon's life. Jon told me that he felt so helpless because he was not able to save Mikey's life in return, and that's why he had taken Mike's death so hard.

The second was seeing a group of three or four young women who had gone to high school with Mike standing off to one side of the room, looking toward Mike and talking among themselves. I asked them if I could do something for them. One said they wanted to pay their respects to Mike but they were scared to walk up to see him. I offered to accompany them to see Mike, and they nodded.

I wrapped my arms around them and escorted them to Mike, where I left them so they could say their goodbyes.

As I turned to leave them, I looked into the casket and saw that Mike was surrounded by cards, notes, medallions, and other tokens of love. We left those with Mike when he was buried.

We had purchased a guestbook for everyone to sign. In retrospect, I was grateful for that: I was in a fog at that time and remembered only a few people I talked with. Looking through the guestbook a few weeks later, I was amazed at all the people who were there that evening. To this day I have no recollection of many who were present. I wanted to thank them all from the bottom of my heart for taking the time to be there to support and love us that evening.

I didn't sleep very much that night. All I could think about was Mike as I replayed moments of his life like scenes from a movie. I thought about his birth, our "surprise" baby like a bonus in addition to Dan and Sean.

I picked up the framed Christmas letter Mike had written to us in December 2005. In it he told us about his life's challenges and how his dad and I had shaped his life up to that point. He was seventeen at the time. That letter still sits on my dresser as a reminder of the Mikey who loved us so much:

> Mom and Dad—you have done more than you will ever know for me. I cannot put a price on all of the things you have done for me or helped me out with. Thank you for everything you have done, some of which you don't even know you have done. Ever since I can remember I have had a feeling of need for you. I remember on my first day of school when I was a kindergartener, even though Mom worked there, I longed to be with you guys. I still get that

feeling; when I'm at school how much I would rather be back in time, holding Dad's hand while you taught me to skate or with you, Mom, picking me up from kindergarten and taking me on a picnic down to the river. The things you did for me when I was younger, the love you showed, even though I might not show it, is in me forever. The way you raised me, all the things you did for me makes me see today what a real loving family is.

Mom and Dad, I love you. You have showed me in all the things you do what loving merciful people are. Spending time with me, talking to me, putting me down to sleep at night, and providing for me, those are things not every child gets. I am so lucky and grateful to have parents like you.

The biggest thing that stands out for me is my fifth-grade year. The toughest year for me by far. Mom, you were going to school and still being a mother, wife, and friend. Dad, you were working to get all the things we have while still being a father, husband, and friend. The things you sacrificed physically and mentally can never be replaced. Mom, you having to leave school early or talking to me late at night when you got home from school and still, after comforting me and calming me down, having to go and do hours of homework. Then, watching me break down and cry the next morning after all the talks we had. Dad, having to watch me pull you, Mom, Dan, and Sean through my hard time must have been extremely hard. I still remember you holding me, not talking, and me feeling like everything was okay for those lucky couple of minutes. My comfort at school was thinking about you taking me fishing, and while I thought about that everything was fine.

> You two did so much for me, Mom, you taking me to see Maureen [a therapist], and Dad, you paying for it. Thank you for everything you put yourself, the family and your friends through during that time. I will never forget that.
>
> You have made me into the person I am today. Looking at your marriage, in a world of divorce and not showing love, I grasp onto everything I see you do. All the sacrifices you made for each other, all the love you show toward each other. That gives me hope and guidance that someday I can have what you do. My greatest thanks go out to the way you raised me, and that someday I can raise my kids with the love, mercy, compassion, and discipline that you have raised me with.
>
> Mom and Dad, I can truly, honestly say that you are the most important people in my life, the people I look up to, and the people I go to for everything. I know that many people do not have one person like that in their life, and I am lucky to have two. I love you guys. Merry Christmas,
> Mike

I set the framed letter back on my dresser.

I wandered into Mike's room and opened each dresser drawer, his scent emanating from his shirts and jeans. In the bottom drawer a small book caught my eye. I picked it up and sat on his bed. There was just enough moonlight coming through his bedroom window to read the opening page. It was Mike's senior high English assignment book of short stories—a miniature memoir of his life up to that point. Mike had written a note in the front expressing his gratitude for all his dad and I had done to help him to graduate in 2007.

I read his foreword out loud:

> This book is dedicated to everyone who helped me graduate. I have a list of people too long to thank, and name-dropping is not my thing. The person who helped me and, more importantly, believed in me when even I did not is my mother, Linda Morrison. I owe more to her than I can put in words, so, Mother, this is for you. For all the time you put into worrying about me getting up on time, getting to school on time, staying in school, getting to all my classes, remembering what assignments I had to do, getting home from school, and actually doing my work. You worked just as hard as I did to help get me where I am, and all my thanks go out to you. I can only hope what you have showed me these past four months I can grasp and live with for the rest of my life. I love you.

Mike had a way with words. He was very sensitive; events in his life touched him in a deep place inside, and he conveyed that depth in the written word.

My mind wandered. *Why did he have to leave me, to leave us? Did he realize the impact his suicide would have on his family and friends?* I missed him so very much. I curled up on his bed under his covers and cried myself to sleep.

Morning came too soon. I was startled by the sound of activity in the hallway. I rolled over and sat up, feeling groggy. Next to my pillow sat Mike's book, a stunning reminder of what day it was.

As I walked into the hallway, I nearly bumped into my sister Tracy as she emerged from the bathroom.

We hugged as tears streamed down our faces.

"Can you help me fix my hair later?" I squeaked out.

Tracy nodded yes.

I placed a kiss on her cheek.

I jumped into the shower before someone else took it. I didn't waste any time in there. When I walked out, the next person was waiting to use it. Everyone needed to be ready to leave the house by nine o'clock. We all wanted to spend a few minutes with Mike before his casket was closed for the final time.

The father of a good friend of our boys, Patrick Loonan, who is a gifted singer-songwriter, wrote this song for Mike after he died.

It's Gonna Be Hard Saying Goodbye to You

Why does it seem the best people we know
are the ones that die first and the bad ones never seem to go?
The drinking and the drugging gonna get its due.
It's gonna be hard saying goodbye to you.

Must be the grim reaper's favorite disease.
Brings the rich the poor and the weak and the strong down to their knees.
Doesn't give a damn who you are or what you do.
It's gonna be hard saying goodbye to you.

You were never alone in your personal hell.
We all went through it with you as well,
hoping and praying that you'd survive and pull through.

It's gonna be hard saying goodbye to you.

Nothing on Earth rivals that terrible sound
as when they put that box into the ground.
We say some prayers and drop a flower or two.
It's gonna be hard saying goodbye to you.

May the trumpets of angels greet your ears;
may they take away your cross and dry your tears.
In the new light of morning, the long night will be through.
It's sure gonna be hard saying goodbye to you.

The funeral was held at a local church we had attended several years earlier, when Mike and Sean were in elementary school. Our family shared a few last moments there with Mike before the casket was closed. Each of us said goodbye to him one more time. When it was my turn, I held Mike's hand and kissed his forehead and cheeks as tears streamed down my face. As I stepped away, I grabbed Allan's hand.

Our family was ushered into a private room for a prayer with Pastor Nate while the attendees found their seats. When it was time, the four of us made the very long, arduous walk down the aisle to the front rows. As I sat there, I could hear the shuffling of feet as people sat down. I heard snippets of conversations, noses being blown, and a few small sobs escaping from those behind us. I remembered my mother's funeral—how surreal it felt hearing the muffled sounds of grief. It was even more surreal now as I looked at Mike's closed casket.

Pastor Nate stood to begin the service. He thanked everyone, on our behalf, for coming to Mike's service. He read the invocation. Then we walked to the pulpit and stood side by side as we each read our tributes to Mike.

Allan started us off: "I want to thank each one of you for coming today. Everyone here feels like family; even if we don't know you well, you knew Mike. Mike would not want us crying today. He would want to hear laughter. Mike was an open book. He would want his story told. Later on, I will share the parts that are the hardest to talk about. That's what Mike would want."

Dan spoke next:

> Mike was always such a special person and made an impression on people his entire life, no matter where he was or where he went. He always shined his big, beautiful eyes at you. He knew if he gave that look and pushed his eyebrows up and down and smiled like only he could, he would get anything he wanted. I'll never forget those looks for the rest of my life. His eye tactics didn't work on everyone, but they always worked on Mom. They were like two peas in a pod. They enjoyed workouts, biking, and hikes, and long and deep conversations. Even during high school, when other kids were too cool to hang with their moms, he was never too cool to hang out with his mom. I have to be honest, sometimes it bothered me the way Mike could look up her with those big blue eyes and get away with murder. Like, if I came home with a C, I would be grounded for a month. If he came home with an F, those two could go out and get DQ and celebrate. All kidding aside, our family was very unique, and the five of us were very close. We spent lots of time together on vacations, camping trips, sports, church (not that any of us

> boys enjoyed that), and frequent trips to see relatives. Our dinner conversations could easily get out of hand and turn disgusting. We always played jokes and poked fun at each other about the clothes we wore, girlfriends, our physical shape, and so on. . . . One time all five of us were driving to my then girlfriend's for dinner. Mike looked up at me and said, "Should we stop and get a feeding trough for her?" Other times I'd give him crap about the swallows tattooed on his arms. Mike was a glowing individual with a heart the size of Colorado. He was physically, mentally, and spiritually strong. He was honest and real. Brother, I will miss you forever, and I love you soooo much.

I stepped up to the microphone next. "Mike was one of the greatest joys of my life, the source of many dear memories and one of the sweetest presents God gave me. I am very proud of him. The struggles he had were real and took me to my knees many times. I always thought he would overcome them. Mike, I could not be more proud of you if I tried. I will carry you in my heart forever and ever until we meet again inside those pearly gates and walk the streets of gold together. I will always love you and be your Mommadukes."

Allan ended his eulogy by sharing in detail about Mike's drug use from beginning to end, concluding,

> Mike had four stars tattooed on his triceps about a year ago. He had two on each arm. He told Linda they represented each of us: Linda, Dan, Sean, and me. . . . Mike was a glass-half-full kind of guy. He was the optimist; he always saw the positive side of people. I have always been the pessimist, and Mike often admonished me for my negativity.

> So, in keeping with that philosophy, I want to end on a positive note. We have lost Mike. We can feel sorry for ourselves and whimper about our loss. Or we can rejoice that God gave us twenty-three years with Mike. Twenty-three great years. I am eternally grateful for this blessing from God. Linda and I don't blame God for the loss of Mike. We believe that God loves us so much that He gave us free will to make our own choices, and He loves us even when we make poor choices. Mike made choices he regretted, but God loved him as much as he does us. I eagerly await the day when I am reunited with Mike in heaven. Mike, I love you.

Sean was not able to speak about his brother during the funeral. I think losing Mike and the closeness they shared was just too much for him. Even now, all these years later, Sean keeps his thoughts and feelings to himself regarding Mike. Sean has shared with me that Mike is his first and last thought each day.

After the service, the pallbearers—Mike's good friends Anthony, Keith, Jon, and Sammy, and Dan and Sean—walked Mike to the hearse. As the door to the hearse was closing, Ruthie, a friend of Mike's from junior high school, ran up to me and handed me a necklace. Through her tears she asked me to put it on Mike's neck, which I did.

We invited family and close friends to the internment at Acacia Park Cemetery. Mike's gravesite is located on a grassy hill that is shaded from the afternoon sun and has a view of the Mississippi River. It was a perfect fit for Mikey, who loved the outdoors. I imagined him looking at the river and the hills that surrounded him. He would love the large oak tree standing over his spot, especially in the autumn when the leaves fall to the ground. When he was a kid, he and Sean loved rolling in fallen leaves.

It was a wonderful send-off. Pastor Nate said a few words and a final prayer. Then everyone placed a flower on his casket before Mike was lowered into the ground.

The most painful part was watching my son being lowered into the hole. It made it real. It made it final. I couldn't imagine leaving my Mikey there, all alone.

At one point I looked at each person standing there, mourning Mike's death. Everyone looked so sad. Like a photo from a camera, that image has stayed with me all these years.

Finally, Allan, Dan, Sean, and I said our last goodbyes to Mike. We turned and walked back to our car.

We returned to the church for a luncheon prepared by friends and women from the church and spent the afternoon sharing a meal and many Mikey stories. I walked around to each table, thanking people for coming. Even in the fog of my grief, I wanted our family and friends to know how much we appreciated their love and support. Everyone lingered well into the afternoon; no one seemed in a hurry to leave. We invited those left to come to our house to share more stories about our son.

Looking back over the years, I believe that outpouring of love and care made the transition into our new life without Mike a little easier. Of course, it didn't take away the pain or sorrow we felt, but it was a cushion we could lean on.

Later that night, around eleven, we heard loud popping

noises coming from the river. Angela called and excitedly told us to go outside and look west.

A large group of Mike's friends were setting off fireworks at the river bluffs. Allan, Brenda, and I ran out to the street just in time to see the last of the fireworks exploding high over the trees. It was a tribute to Mike from his close friends.

The next morning, I opened the blinds in our upstairs family room. In the middle of the street sat the neighborhood cat that would show up from time to time on our back deck, curled up on one of the deck chairs. We knew he lived in the neighborhood and appeared well taken care of, but we didn't know the cat's real name; he had solid black fur without any markings, so we called him Blackie. It wasn't a very creative name, but it worked for us.

Mike was an animal lover. He always begged us to get him a dog, which we never did. Whenever Blackie showed up on the deck, Mikey would sit next to him and stroke his fur, enjoying that contented purr. Yet Blackie had a mind of his own; it was always on his terms. Some days he would let you pet him. Other times he'd just as quickly bite you, jump down, and be gone. Not a hard bite, not the kind that breaks the skin, but one that let you know he was finished being petted.

Mike tried several times to hold Blackie as he petted him, but Blackie would jump down from Mike's arms and dart away. This went on for several years. Sometimes the cat wouldn't show up for weeks or months at a time, and we'd wonder to each other whether Blackie was still in the neighborhood. Then, out of the blue, he'd show up.

That morning Blackie sat still as a statue in the middle

of our street, looking very regal. The thought crossed my mind that he was like a sentry guarding us, looking out for us in Mike's absence. I watched him for several minutes. Could Blackie sense Mike had departed from us? I'd like to think he knew something had happened to Mikey. I walked away to attend to a couple things, and when I went back to the window a while later he was gone. I never did see Blackie again after that.

19. The Lives He Touched

Over the next few days, we said more goodbyes as family and friends returned home and resumed their lives. Jon ferried those who needed rides back to the airport. Sammy was the last of Mike's out-of-town friends to depart after the funeral.

I began my journey to find my "new normal" in the days and weeks after the funeral. Allan remembers the week or two following Mike's death as a whirlwind of activity. We were trying so hard to honor Mike at his visitation and funeral. Of course, funerals aren't for the dead: they are for those of us left behind to grieve. But that temporary distraction had been a hidden blessing. It delayed the true grieving process for a time and gave us a short period in which to slide more gently into grief.

That distraction had now evaporated. It was time for our family to start the real grieving process alone in our empty house, without a church full of friends and family. I walked aimlessly through the house many times each day, usually ending up in Mike's room. I felt peaceful and comfortable there. I would look through his dresser drawers, caressing his clothing. I picked up T-shirts, searching for a whiff of his scent. In one of his drawers he had loose change, baseball cards in a case, and a silver Mercedes car emblem, which no doubt he broke off a car. He had an old camera with pictures of people I didn't recognize. He had a couple old cell phones and a stethoscope he'd purchased when he was training to become an EMT. I would sit or lie down on his bed, curling up in the comforter he and I had purchased together. I felt his spirit with me, giving me comfort. I wanted to leave his room just as it was before his death. Going through his things was something Allan and I would need to do . . . later.

The next task was reading through the more than two hundred sympathy cards and letters we'd received. Allan and I sat in the dining room, reading through each one and making note of who sent cards and memorials, flowers and meals we received, and the many ways in which people had reached out to us during the past couple weeks.

I kept each card and letter we received. Many came from people we didn't know but who knew Mikey. He knew people from all over the country because of the many treatment centers he had been in. We felt especially touched by the cards and letters from his friends in Carbondale. Some contained just a few sentences, while others ran to several paragraphs or even multiple pages, sharing how people met Mike, how he affected their lives, and condolences to us. Reading through them still brings tears to my eyes and joy to my heart. We were blessed with an amazing young man who changed so many lives in the short time he walked this earth. The following excerpts give a small taste of the impact Mike had on those who knew him:

I met Mike at City Market. It is rare in life to meet someone like Mike—young or old, from whatever walk of life. Mike was everyone's friend. I don't know that I will ever again meet someone I believe in so completely. I hope my children grow to possess the same beautiful passion for life, people, and friendship that Mike has. Please know that his spirit lives on in all of us. His beauty will always brighten our days. And I am a better person for knowing him. —Brian

I remember his bright blue eyes, his infectious grin and boundless energy clearly. He had a way of making me feel like I was his best friend. Everyone who met him felt the same way after a few minutes. His honesty, openness, and willingness to share his thoughts, feelings, and experiences here [at Hazelden] were unparalleled. His intellect/curiosity never ceased to amaze me. Also know that many, including me, cared for and loved Mike. To a person, all who knew him here at Hazelden and I'm sure from Colorado to Minnesota, would give him any gift—physical, emotional, spiritual, or otherwise without a second thought. —Vernon

Friday night I just couldn't fall asleep. The news of Mikey kept me awake. Also, as a mom, my heart was aching for all of you. I prayed and prayed and prayed some more—as hard as I could—that God would find a way to let everyone and especially his family know he was okay. I finally drifted off to sleep as the sun was coming up. The next day Juliana called me. "I had a dream about Mike," she said. "He wanted me to know he was okay, and he wanted his mom to know he was okay. He said he made his mom wake up in the middle of the night and look out the window so she would see baby bunnies and that would let her know 'I am okay.'" I just wanted to let you know, I think God wants us to know, Mikey is doing okay. —Carrie

In the short time we had together at Hazelden I can truly say I loved Mike like a brother. His smile and energy filled up the room every day, and I wouldn't have made it through treatment without him. While we only had one month together, I feel like I have known him my whole life. I will never forget his smile and great presence and would do anything I can to help your family through this time. Much love, Scott

No matter the mood I was in, whenever I saw him, he put a smile on my face. He could brighten a room with one smile. He will be missed every day. —Ashley

Mike was truly a light + an emotional gravity. His personality brought many people to him, and he was naturally the center of attention. My favorite memories are of him laughing and finding humor in anything, him scaling the tree @ the BWCA to hang our food pack, and teaching me to drive Dan's jeep. His loss is great for us left behind. —Holly

I have this picture in my head of Jesus & Mike walking and talking together. I can see Mike telling Jesus about CrossFit and the amazing way his body was made to do such difficult things. Jesus smiles at the compliment but smiles even more as Mike tells Him of the wonderful love he had from his family & what a blessing you all were to him during his short time on Earth. I can't wait for the day when you'll see Mike again and he'll tell you that himself. —Cindy

Mike had glow to him, a great attitude about life, as well a great work ethic for AA and NA programs. He was willing to do anything to stay sober. He came into my life at the perfect time when I needed someone with his positive energy the most. I feel truly blessed I was able to meet such a strong, caring, and uplifting individual. RIP MIKE —Troy

For a week after Mike's funeral, Allan and I sat in our dining room, writing card after card. There were so many people to thank. In addition to those who sent memorials and flowers, I had friends who had cleaned my house, weeded my gardens, and brought meals for us. Three longtime friends purchased a pink rosebush in memory of Mike and attached a card reading, "The pink rose means gentleness, grace, joy, and sweetness. We can't think of better words to describe Mike." That rosebush has bloomed beautifully every summer since his death.

My sister-in-law Lori had paper products, disposable dining ware, and coffee beans delivered to us—something she had particularly appreciated when a friend did it for her after the death of her husband, Michael, a few years earlier. Another friend, Mary, breezed into our house the day she learned of Mike's death bearing three cases of water and several twelve-packs of soda pop. She gave me a hug and said a few words of comfort and breezed out. She had lost her husband, Marshall, to a brain tumor in October 2010 and her son, Devon—also a good friend of Mikey's—six months later in a tragic swimming accident. Those two acts of love from women who knew and understood our pain will forever be etched in my heart.

On July 3, 2012, twelve days after Mike died, I began keeping a journal. It opens,

> I am so sad tonight. I miss Mikey so much. It's such an overwhelming feeling, this grief. Tonight, Allan and I watched a movie; I don't remember it, but I felt so sad afterward. Allan held me while I cried and cried and cried. My heart hurts as I think of him. He was such a beautiful boy who turned into an awesome young man. I know his struggles were great. So great he couldn't conquer them. I know in my heart he didn't want to leave us. He felt so hopeless—he was so tortured by his addiction. Only God knows his true pain. I hope and pray God met him in that room where he overdosed. My wounded warrior. I pray that Mike found his peace in the arms of Jesus. No more pain, no more sorrow. His struggle is over. Seeing Blackie that morning after Mikey's funeral comforted me, as he sat right in front of our house in the middle of the street standing guard, watching and looking over Mikey's family and his car. My grief is lessened by crying, by watching Mike's DVD from the funeral, and writing in my journal. Someday I will see him and hold him and tell him I love him. For now, I will miss him. I will remember the good times, the times he made me laugh, his smile that lit up his face, and his sparkling baby-blue eyes. I'll see him again.

In Mike's obituary we had asked that memorials be given to Project Turnabout. A couple weeks after Mike's funeral,

Allan and I drove to Granite Falls to present the center with a check. In the end, we had raised three thousand dollars.

The staff and its directors hosted a luncheon for us and gave us a tour of the facility. It was bittersweet to be back there. The CEO was very gracious and grateful for our contribution. We asked that it be used to help those coming into treatment without means to pay. It was just a fraction of the actual cost, but we hoped the donations would help those in greatest need.

20. Live Like You Have No Idea When God's Calling Your Number

In mid-August Allan and I drove to Colorado to clean out Mike's storage unit. It was crammed full of totes, boxes, and brown paper sacks of Mike's belongings. We went through it all and made three piles: items to dispose of, items we wanted to give to Mike's friends, and items we wanted to keep. The first thing I saw was a life-size stuffed gorilla that Mike brought with him from Minnesota. I think he'd won it at the State Fair. It currently sits on a recliner in his bedroom. We gave his skis to his best friend, Jordan. There were boxes filled with books, clothes, and the many household items he had collected while living in Carbondale. He had more than twenty Beanie Babies—I'd had no idea he collected them, and many I still have in my possession. Basketball and hockey jerseys he had collected over the years. A red wig for Halloween, a couple of cowboy hats and belt buckles. Who would have thought he was such a cowpoke?

In the storage unit were the mattress and box spring Mike had moved with him since his early days in Carbondale. Allan remembered how careful Mike was in unloading his mattress and box spring, which had puzzled Allan a bit. Mike wanted to make sure they didn't damage it. After Mike died, Rob from CrossFit explained that Mike was hopping from place to place in his early days in Carbondale, usually crashing on friends' couches. Rob told Mike that a man needs his own bed, a place of his own to lay his head. Mike had left Minnesota with only a carload of his things. He liked his privacy, and I imagine couch surfing got old for him. I believe that Rob's recommendation made so much sense to Mikey that he went out and purchased the bed and took special care of it for every move after that.

We hated to donate the set, but we couldn't keep it. It was bittersweet for me when we dropped it off at the Salvation Army Store—another piece of my Mike and his story going in a new direction.

In a small plastic tote that he had painted camouflage green we found his high school yearbooks, Pokémon and baseball card collections, several of the big bling watches that he loved to wear, pictures from high school, and a digital camera that had a few pictures of Mike and some friends.

Most surprising of all was a brown paper bag filled with cards and letters he'd received over the years from family and friends during the times he was in treatment or newly released. I read through a few:

> Keep up the good work. Love, Aunt H

> Mike, Life is the journey—sometimes it's great, sometimes

> we get detoured. Know you are on the right road. Love and prayers, Ginny
>
> Mike! I know that you can lick this thing. You have the "guts" to do it, but it's up to you. I will always think of you as one of my best friends. Take care of yourself! Good luck. Gordy

I cried as I realized how deeply sentimental a soul he was. Few glimpsed this tenderness.

We slowly made our way through the unit, laughing sometimes at the things he'd kept and the way he packed his boxes. I remember pulling out a baseball hat, putting it on, and cocking it off to one side, and striking a pose imitating his badass tough-guy look. Humor helped the ache inside of me. By the time we finished cleaning out the unit, every nook and cranny of our car was stuffed with Mike's things. Then we drove to Carbondale.

On August 18, we gathered at Sopris Park with Mike's Carbondale friends for a community hike up Mushroom Rock and a picnic in his honor. Allan and I knew very little of the life Mike had made for himself in Carbondale, and we did not yet know that the people who loved our son would soon become an intricate part of our lives.

Mike's friends Brenda and Jo had organized this event. Brenda had put a notice in the local paper about Mike, the hike, and the picnic, and Jo had enlisted many people to help organize the day. When we arrived, Jo, Rob, Jordan, and Jen were setting up for the picnic. Other friends had set up a sound system with a microphone, a DVD player, and a large-screen TV.

After everyone arrived, we all made the short drive to Red Hill, the start of our hike. Some of Mike's CrossFit buddies jogged from the park to the parking lot where we met and continued their jog up to Mushroom Rock. I think twenty-five or thirty people made the hike.

Several people wore the memorial T-shirts and wristbands that Lauren and Angela, two of Mike's closest friends, had designed. The shirts came in two styles. The black shirt had his full name, Michael Thomas Morrison, his birth and death dates 8.8.88–6.21.12, and his mantra, "Always live like we have no idea when God is going to call our number," on the front side and *MIKEY MO #14*, the number from his hockey jersey, on the backside. The second style was a white shirt with his full name, birth and death dates, and a picture of his smiling face on the front and his mantra on the back. The red wristbands had his initials, MTM, and birth and death dates.

It was a joyful time, with lots of laughter and stories about Mike. I remember talking with different groups of Mike's friends as we made our way up the hill. There was this quietness when we reached the top of Mushroom Rock. Perhaps some of us were reflecting on good times with Mikey or thinking about his crazy antics, and we all silently grieved his death as we looked over Carbondale, which had become so ingrained in him. I was grieving for my son and the times he and I had stood on this same rock, and at the same time I marveled at this group of people who'd become my son's family and now mine. I don't remember how long we stood there, but after a time we headed back down the hill.

We spent the afternoon with close to one hundred of our new friends. So many people talked to us: Jordan, Troy, Brenda, Frazier, Carter, Jennifer, Lynn, Shaggi and his family, Brisa and her daughter and granddaughter, to name just a few. We began to understand how much Mikey was loved by so many: customers and coworkers from City Market, his CrossFit family, and members of his AA and NA groups. He had a positive influence on so many people in the town. Mike's friends from CrossFit told us they were going to establish a scholarship in Mike's honor. Allan and I played the DVD from the funeral, and then we read the eulogies from the funeral. After that, people shared their stories in person or handed us written accounts of how they met Mike. This helped us fill in what we didn't know about Mike's life in Carbondale.

Kelly, who had met Mike through AA meetings at St. Paul Sober Living, sponsored Mike but also learned a lot from him about his own recovery. He shared,

> Mike had some very happy times in recovery here in the Roaring Fork Valley. The people he touched are too many to mention. There was the recovery community, his co-workers, the CrossFit crowd, and all the customers at City Market that he helped have a brighter day. He loved to fish, ride bikes, and hike. I know he recognized God in all things through our discussions. God was always there if you needed Him and comforted those in need.
>
> I have an experience that needs to be shared. I received a

call one night from a friend who said a friend of ours was drunk and had taken a bunch of pills to kill himself. This man didn't like me very much, so I asked Mike to go with us to help us. When we got to this man's house, he refused to go to the hospital. Mike talked to him for an hour while we made sure this man didn't have a gun hidden in the house to hurt himself. When we got back to them, Mike had talked him into going to the hospital. He would only go if Mike drove him there. Mike drove him to Glenwood and stayed with him until 3:00 a.m. even though he had to work in the morning. The man recovered and is alive today. To be able to help another suffering soul was an experience that carried him for months to follow.

Another good friend, Brian, told us,

I met Mike at City Market. I was immediately drawn to this young man with this amazing positive energy. Mike and I also worked out at CrossFit. Mike was an inspiration to so many of us, and in CrossFit he was unparalleled. I had never seen anyone in a workout give so much. Like Tony Robbins, Mike taught us when you think you have given your all, you can always reach down deep and find more. It is rare in life to meet someone like Mike. Young or old, from whatever walk of life, Mike was everyone's friend. I don't know that I will ever again meet someone I believe in so completely. Please know that his spirit lives on in all of us. His beauty will always brighten our days. I am a better person for knowing him.

Mike's friend Troy said, "I just wanted to let you know that Mikey was a big part of my recovery and sobriety. I truly loved him. It was great to work, fish, and live with him. I will miss him a lot. I do know that I wouldn't be where I am today without Mike's help."

At the end of the picnic, Brenda came walking across the parking lot with a hundred red and blue helium balloons in hand. I thought she might just fly away! I ran up to grab a few from her hand. She had brought pens, pencils, and paper for anyone who wanted to write a note to Mike and attach it to a balloon. We sat or stood at the picnic tables, writing our notes. As each person finished, I watched them attach the note to a balloon and release it. Soon the sunny blue sky above was awash with our balloons, notes dangling from their ribbons. It was a beautiful sight as they floated higher and higher, going in different directions as the wind caught them. It was the perfect ending to the celebration of our son's life with his Colorado family.

Afterward we met with several of Mike's friends at a bar in town, and though we were not drinking, we enjoyed the informal remembrances of Mike's life. One story sticks out in particular. Rob had given Mike an expensive watch for Christmas. There was one stipulation: if Mike relapsed and planned to pawn the watch, Rob wanted it returned. One morning, several months later, Rob found the watch sitting on his desk at CrossFit.

On our last evening in Carbondale, a group of us went for dinner at the White House, where we had eaten many meals on our visits with Mike. Several patrons came by to offer us their condolences. The next morning was difficult for me; Mike's time there was over, and now we were leaving the Colorado family we had just gotten to know. I cried as we left town, not wanting to leave, yet wanting to get home to see Dan and Sean and tell them about our trip. Our car was fully packed with the remainder of Mike's belongings and our hearts full of memories.

At home with Dan and Sean, we tried to explain the love we felt in Carbondale and the life Mike had established there in the last two years of his life. His charismatic personality and zest for life had changed that community, and its people had reciprocated with overwhelming love and support for him and, in turn, for us.

21. Light One Candle for Mike

After Mike died, I was told that grief sneaks up on you. It will overwhelm you when you least expect it. Yes, that is very true. It is a moment-by-moment experience. Those first few weeks and months ebbed and flowed. One day I'd be going about my daily routine and have little sorrow. The next day I could be completely swept away by my grief.

I had my first experience of a sneak attack in early December 2012. I remember it vividly. I drove to work, singing along to Christmas CDs. I was feeling happy. My day went well as I roomed my patients at the clinic where I was working, joking with my coworkers and making small talk with the doctors. I was walking toward my desk when I literally felt a veil drop over me. I was suddenly overwhelmed with grief, a sadness I had no control over. I sat down hard in my chair with tears spilling down my cheeks. My heart pounded, and I had a hard time breathing. I sat at my desk, trying to compose myself—trying to understand what was happening. Finally, I realized what had just happened. Grief had just snuck up on me. Knowing what I was experiencing helped. I was glad I was at work that day because I didn't have time to stop and grieve. I returned to my tasks, and slowly my sorrow eased. But the experience made me realize how fragile I was and that this journey was not yet over.

My life was deeply altered by Mike's death, but the world doesn't stand still. Most of my friends, no matter how understanding and compassionate they were, had never experienced anything like this. They moved on, as they should.

I stood in these shadows for a long time, watching their lives go on. It was hard to attend those firsts after Mike's death: baby showers, wedding showers, weddings and receptions, graduations, all those major life events. Over time the pain lessened, and I could engage in those events with less sadness and eventually with true joy. With each passing year it gets easier and I find myself looking forward to celebrating these life events.

Everyone grieves differently. Some, like me, stand in the shadows as they grapple with this new life before slowly stepping into the light again. Others jump back into life quickly, wanting to put the experience behind them. And there are some who, no matter how hard they try, remain but a skeleton of their former selves. There is no framework for this. Each person can only begin to participate in life when they're ready.

Of course I wish Mike were here to celebrate with his friends and ours, but he is not. I know he would not want us to continue to mourn his passing. As he said in his last note to us, *I lived life to the fullest, experienced so many heart-touching moments, and lived in a world of love from you. Live your lives as you always have, and don't stop being yourselves.* So that is what I try to do each day: live my life to the fullest, seek out moving moments, and love freely. I began doing it for Mike, and now I do it for me.

On a sunny Saturday morning in July, Dan, Sean, Jon, Allan, and I drove up to Jon's cabin on Clear Lake. We celebrated Mike's life by planting a shrub Jon had purchased for the occasion. Each of us took a turn with the shovel, scooping out dirt, and planted it. Then we each helped fill up the hole and watered it. The five of us gathered around that small shrub and bowed our heads as I said a short prayer. We all felt a little sad as we thought of honoring Mikey with this gift. Our moods lightened as we went fishing for the afternoon on Jon's pontoon. I can't remember if we caught anything. The time we spent together that day was very special, fish or no fish.

That August 8 would have been Mike's twenty-fourth birthday, our first without him. Allan put a birthday notice in the local paper, the *Pioneer Press* (as we continue to do for each of his birthdays and his anniversary date).

Later that morning I drove an hour and a half to Happily Ever After Tattoos in Harris, Minnesota, where I met my sister Tracy and we had tattoos done in honor of our dad and Mike. The artist, Adam, had done several of my tattoos and helped design this one for my abdomen. It consists of four stars, one for each of my three sons plus Jon, who is like a son to me; two butterflies that represent my dad and Allan; two flowers for my sisters; two entwined hearts for my mom and stepmom; and swirl designs around Mike's and my dad's birth and death dates. It is a beautiful tattoo that reminds me every day of my precious son.

Then Allan and I met Sean, Dan, and Jon at the cemetery. Everyone brought flowers, and we placed them all around Mikey's spot. I had bought a helium balloon and two solar lights that I put in the ground on either side of his headstone. For a gravesite, it looked very festive. Another family friend, Zack, arrived with his then girlfriend, Becky, which was a pleasant surprise. We sang "Happy Birthday" to Mike and hung out for a while.

After Zack and Becky departed, the five of us went to a Mexican restaurant for a quiet dinner and then went to our homes. Later that evening, Allan and I agreed that the day hadn't been as sad as we thought it was going to be. For me, the days leading up to his birthday had been harder. Yes, we missed him, and we loved him, but we knew Mike was at peace. God's strength was surrounding us. We could also feel the power of so many people praying for us. In a journal entry from 2012, I wrote, *Thank you, God, for comforting me through this time. Without You, I do not know how I would have the strength to do this. You are my strength, solace, and source of life. Jesus, thank you for your love, your sacrificial death and resurrection. I do love you so.*

The first holiday that arrived was Thanksgiving. In the past, our table had been full of food with family and friends gathered around. But, as a family, we decided not to invite anyone over that year. Our day was very somber. I cooked my usual dinner of a stuffed turkey, mashed potatoes, candied yams, cranberry salad, dinner rolls, and pumpkin pie for dessert. We sat at the table, talking about insignificant things, but my heart was missing my boy. I realized that no one had mentioned Mikey at all that day, including me. I felt that, somehow, we had betrayed him. I determined that the next Thanksgiving would be different.

And it was. The next year I told everyone that I wanted each of us to share a humorous memory of Mikey at dinner. I started us off by remembering the time he ran downstairs, pointed to a big red ring around his mouth, and told me he thought he had a disease. I told him, "It looks like you had a glass stuck on your mouth." He guffawed and blushingly said, "Oh yeah, I did." We all had a good laugh. The laughs continued as the guys shared their memories. By the end of the meal we were talking and laughing about Mikey and his antics. It was a very gratifying feeling for me.

For our first Christmas, I think the best descriptive word is *rote*. We put up our tree and decorated the house, but we found no joy or pleasure in doing it. On Christmas morning we opened gifts as usual, yet it was with a sense of sadness. Sean and I stood in front of the Christmas tree as we clung to each other and cried. We felt a gaping, bleeding hole in our hearts that day. Still, that was the Christmas that Allan came up with the idea for each of us to light a candle and then together light one candle for Mike as a reminder that he is still here with us in spirit. The candles stayed lit all day. It is a wonderful tradition we have continued.

The weekend of June 20 to 24, 2013, Mike's one-year anniversary, Allan reserved a houseboat for us on Lake Vermillion. It was a time for us to bond as a family and make new memories. We wanted to relax and let go of some of the stress of the past year, and we had a delightful time. We fished almost every waking moment. Allan caught his first muskie. When I wasn't fishing, I was reading books and sunbathing. We swam in the lake (which I am not fond of doing). In the evenings we barbecued dinners while we relaxed, watching the sunset. Sometimes we played card games or just sat quietly, looking out on the lake, as the dark encased us. We made that memorial trip for two years after Mike died.

Mikey's 2013 birthday was a little less eventful. We went to his grave as a family and then went out to dinner at Applebee's. It was a cloudy evening; while we were waiting on our food to arrive, there was a lightning strike and a big clap of thunder, and the power went off in the restaurant. We ate dinner by the light coming through the window. Perhaps Mike was playing a practical joke on us.

In spring 2014, as I was cleaning the house, I thought about this journey I had been on for the past year and a half. A thought struck me like a lightning bolt: my son was going to be gone from me forever. FOREVER! I just could not wrap my heart around that thought. I called my dear friend Kristina, whose son, Cooper, had died a year and a half before Mike.

"Hey, Kris," I asked, "do you have a minute to talk?"

"Of course I do. What's up?"

"I just had a thought that ripped through me. Have you been able to comprehend that Cooper is going to be gone forever?"

"No, it's too overwhelming."

"Kris, this is forever and ever and ever! How do you get through it? And how can I be without Mikey the rest of my life?" Tears streamed down my face.

Gently and quietly she said, "I know, I get it. It is beyond our understanding. My faith helps me so much. But yeah, sistah, I totally understand."

We chatted a bit longer before we hung up. Our discussion didn't take away the heart-shaped hole in me, but by knowing that she understood what I was feeling and empathized with me, I somehow felt strangely comforted.

Each holiday, birthday, and anniversary of Mike's death has gotten a little easier for us. The intense grief has lessened. The deep sorrow I felt in those first couple of years has loosened its hold on me. However, I will always wish he could still be here with us, sober or not.

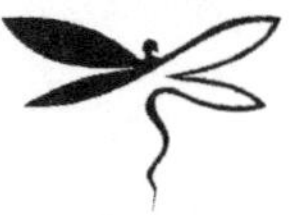

Epilogue

I lay my pen to rest on the paper. I let out a deep sigh. I envision Michael smiling down on me. I have told his story and woven mine into it. The two make one.

His voice echoes in my mind: "You did it, Mom. You shared my story. I can see you've grown through the pain I left you in. You have lived well despite all I have put you through." I have felt his presence whispering in my ear as I wrote, sharing comments, thoughts, memories, and stories of his life I'd forgotten.

Death changes you. You cannot go back to being the same person you were. After the death of my child, that Linda no longer exists. Whether it's a spouse, your mom or dad, a dream you had, or when you hear those words "terminal cancer," you are changed.

I changed the moment the police officer said to me, "I am sorry to inform you of the death of your son Mike." At that precise moment, I felt my life fold up on me, turn me upside down and inside out, and spew me out headlong into a life that no longer felt safe and secure. Loss, sorrow, and grief change you—not momentarily but forever. The phrase "the dark night of the soul" is precisely what I felt for a very long time.

I may look the same, smile the same smile, or laugh at your jokes. I may even look like I am engaged in conversation, but I am often "gone." Sometimes I get lost in my thoughts as something triggers a memory of Mikey, and suddenly, I am no longer present in the conversation. I have had friends tell me, "It's good to have the old you back." Inside I laugh a harsh laugh. I want to say to them, "No I'm not back. I'm not coming back—ever! I can't when I'm learning to live without an integral appendage."

Yet I feel a new me emerging, one who is willing to step out of the shadows of grief and reconnect with the world around me. I am more reflective and introspective. I feel more deeply. Life is more sacred, and I am more attuned to it. I no longer sweat the small stuff—really, it's all small.

Every day I live with a heart-shaped hole inside my heart. In the first months that hole was gaping and bleeding. Even as people around me got up and went to work, to baseball games or concerts or out for lunch—all things I used to do without thinking about it—I couldn't do even one without feeling completely drained of energy. One minute I'd be holding it together, and the next minute I'd break down sobbing. I couldn't imagine how I was ever going to feel whole again.

In fall 2012 I had received a text from Mike's friend Lauren. She said that when I felt ready, she would like to have me come to Welcome Manor, the treatment facility where she worked, and share Mike's story. I replied that I would like to do that and I'd let her know when I was ready. In spring 2013 I called Lauren to tell her I thought I was ready to come and speak. She set a date and time for me to come, and I began to prepare my talk.

I started making notes. I couldn't share Mike's story without sharing my story as well. The two stories are intricately woven together. Sharing my story that first time was very difficult, but at the same time it was cathartic. I believe that is when the hole in my heart found its first healing moment. I have since shared our story at Welcome Manor two or three times a year, and each time brings a little more healing for my heart.

I strongly believe that I have to be intentional about the things I do that help me heal. I have two choices: stay in bed, pull the covers over my head, continue grieving my loss, and live a life of darkness, pain, and sorrow—or acknowledge my sorrow and pain and then choose to get up, shower, dress, and move forward through my day. I have chosen option number two. It is not easy or comfortable, but I am moving slowly toward the light that brings healing. Each day gets a tiny bit easier. Don't get me wrong: I miss Mikey every single day, and I always will. Yet I know that Mike would not want me to continue to grieve for him. He would want me to live fully each day, despite my sorrow. And that's what I try to do—every day.

One of Mike's favorite sayings when I complained to him about things in my life was "Don't be all butthurt, Mom." Thinking of him saying that makes me smile and encourages me to live each day to the fullest. It is my gift to him and to myself, and it becomes another healing moment for my heart.

I visit Mike's gravesite weekly. I usually bring flowers

for the vase by his grave marker and spend a few minutes telling him about my week and anything going on in our family or in our country. I decorate his spot seasonally for his birthday, Thanksgiving, Christmas, and Valentine's Day. My good friend Carol made Mike a Thanksgiving wreath and a huge Christmas wreath that I place by his marker. I bought a small Christmas tree that I bring out to his spot and decorate with ornaments from his childhood and that his friends have brought. Perhaps that's a little macabre, but it brings another piece of healing to my heart.

At Christmastime 2019, Dan brought his baby son out to visit Mike. They left a penguin ornament on his tree with a beautiful personal sentiment from Dan written on the back side. Still, I cried at this reminder that we are still living without Mikey.

I now travel to Colorado every year to visit Mike's friends. I hike up Mushroom Rock and look out over Carbondale, the town he loved and where he made so many friends—friends who have become my friends. Being up there brings another piece of healing to my heart.

I think of putting my heart back together like a mosaic of small pieces of colored glass, arranged into patterns and held together by the adhesive of love and the grout of tears. Each healing moment helps complete this beautiful puzzle. Moments can be meticulously arranged or mysteriously placed. My heart's hole gets smaller with each tick of the clock because I am encircled by the love and support of family and friends and the healing balm of God's love and goodness. There is a vibrant richness about me I didn't possess before. I feel stronger, like a butterfly that struggled to emerge from her cocoon but was birthed into a new life and released from the grip of death. I feel a fearlessness as I move forward in my life and a tenderness that comes from living without my child. I am not the person I once was, but I hope others like who I am becoming. I really do.

Acknowledgments

I am very grateful to the team at Wise Ink Creative Publishing, especially Dara M. Beevas, its cofounder and CEO. The first time I talked to her about writing this book, she was nothing but supportive. She spent over an hour and a half on the phone with me, listening to my story. She had no reason to talk to a random person calling about her son's story. I've felt a deep connection to her from that first conversation. She tells me how special my story is when I doubt it. She and the staff at Wise Ink have been amazing. Writing a book is no small task: it's hard. There are so many avenues to go down, but Dara has navigated with me down each roadway. My fears, worries, and concerns have been taken seriously, and she has relieved my anxiety on many occasions. We have had deep conversations about my story, our lives and the ever-changing world we live in.

Dara, thank you from the bottom of my heart.

I have had the pleasure of two incredible editors. My first was Cole Nelson, who walked me through two edits of my manuscript. He left Wise Ink before I completed my book, but his skill and expertise made me a better writer. Thank you, Cole.

My second editor, Kellie M. Hultgren of KMH Editing,

has been fabulous. We have been through three edits of my book. Each edit has been thorough, precise and in-depth. Kellie has a knack with words and ideas and getting me to dig deep inside. Our first meeting was on Zoom, and from the moment we began talking about the book, I knew she was the right editor for me. We clicked. She answers my questions, takes my calls, and has passed on to me a wealth of knowledge that has made the final copy of *Dear Heroin* so incredible. Kellie, thank you so very much.

It has been a pleasure (mostly—did I mention writing a book is hard?) to work with these two amazing women. I am indebted to both of them. They have incredible experience and a set of skills that this budding author has relied on so very much. Again, thank you both so very much.

Another major player I want to thank is Patrick Maloney, production director at Wise Ink. He took the interior of my book and worked his magic adding designs, pictures, and chapter motifs. Each page has come to life. Thank you, Patrick, for your skill, expertise and flair in making the interior amazing.

I want to thank Graham Warnken, production editor and a member of our team who is supporting us. He has coordinated each phase of the publication. He has managed the publishing staff, editing content and approves final layouts. He is supporting us as we begin distribution. Thank you, Graham, so very much.

What is a book without a title page? I have had the pleasure of working with Emily Mahon, graphic designer. A Philadelphia native who worked at Doubleday as their Art Director, her work has been honored with awards from AIGA, The

Type Director's Club, The Art Director's Club and The New York Book Show. She had been published in 50 Books/50 Covers, TDC Annuals, Communication Arts, Graphis and Print, among others. Emily designed nine covers for me to choose from. Each one was a work of art. I was so amazed by her designs. I had such a hard time selecting a book cover that I queried more than forty friends and family members as to their top three choices. Of course, there were several covers that were tied for top spot, but my favorite was number one and as they say, the rest is history. Emily, you are an incredible artist and graphic designer. I could not have chosen a better artist to capture the essence and heart of *Dear Heroin*. I absolutely love the cover. Thank you so very much.

I want to thank Katharine Bolin, marketing strategist and founder of Sweet Reach Media LLC. Your expertise in web design has been incredible. I was really intimidated by all the aspects of setting up a website. You expertly walked me through it. I love my author website. You made it look easy, Katie. Thank you so much.

I want to thank Peter Blau, instructor at the Loft Literary Center in Minneapolis. When I took my first writing class in the spring of 2014, I was anxious and nervous. His class introduction was "have fun, learn a bit, and just write." From my first five minutes in class, I knew I had taken the right class. Peter's calming presence and reassuring words gave me the courage to write. Without that, I doubt I would have continued. Peter, I am indebted to you for your encouragement and helping me realize I can write. I'm forever grateful to you.

I want to thank Patricia Hoolihan, author, writer, and

teacher at the Loft. I have had the privilege of taking several of her classes. What began as a student/teacher relationship shifted to a friendship that has continued. Patricia gave me wise counsel on my manuscript, and she did several readings of my book including some insightful edits. After the last set of edits, she told me she'd taken me as far as she could and I would need more professional editing. She graciously wrote a heartfelt endorsement for Dear Heroin. We have continued meeting, grabbing coffee or lunch, and chatting about our lives as writers, women, and grandmothers. I am so very grateful that I had her as an instructor and for the knowledge and experience she was willing to share with a newbie author. Patricia, thank you from the bottom of my heart.

A big shout out to William Kent Krueger, author of *Ordinary Grace*, *This Tender Land*, the Cork O'Connor Mystery Series, and many others. Thank you for taking the time to share a beer and some of your story with me. Thank you for listening to Mike's story and answering the long list of questions I had about being a writer and author. It was an honor and pleasure to spend time in the company of such a well-known author. You are one of the kindest and most humble men I know. Thank you, Kent.

I want to thank Gloria Englund, founder of Recovering U and author of *Living in the Wake of Addiction: Lessons for Courageous Caregivers*, for reading my manuscript and sharing her valuable experience on addiction recovery and support and keeping me current in the latest recovery language. We share a grief few mothers experience, and in the aftermath we a share a message of hope to others walking this path. I think Aaron and Mike are very proud of us. I am very grateful to you.

I want to thank Colleen Szot, bestselling author of *Christian Wives: The Women Behind the Evangelists,* seven years named "Writer of the Year" for Direct Response, thirty-two Addy Awards, 2018 Advertising Hall of Fame inductee, and several other outstanding awards, for reading my manuscript and editing several chapters. Your expertise has enhanced my book. Thank you so much.

How do you get a person to endorse your book? Well, you ask them to. I want to thank four special people that have endorsed my book. First, Richard Bahr. I met Richard through a friend of a friend. Our first meeting was at the Mall of America. We spent about a half an hour trying to find each other. I didn't know there was more than one Starbucks there. Once we finally met up, it was a four-hour meeting. Richard is a life-long resident of Minnesota. He was president of and a partner in a successful manufacturing firm. He has a passion for service and has been involved with organizations that provide a "second chance" to those in need. He co-founded a social ministry with his wife, Carla, called Threshold to New Life, which gives assistance to those at risk of losing housing, effectively reducing homelessness. He is a published author of *Amazed: Why the Humanity of Jesus Matters* and *Those People: The True Character of the Homeless.* Richard is a very caring man with a heart for those in need. We talked a little about his story and I told him about Mikey. He graciously read my manuscript and wrote a moving endorsement for *Dear Heroin.* Richard, thank you for being real, honest and doing the work you do.

Next, I want to thank Judith Sullivan, author of *The Terrifying Wind: Seeking Shelter Following the Death of a Child.* I met her at a book reading she was hosting in St. Paul. I was moved by her story. I shared a bit of my story with her and she asked me to keep in touch with her as I continued to write my book. We met again, shortly after I finished my manuscript. I asked if she would write an endorsement for my book, to which she immediately responded "yes". Her heartfelt endorsement means so much to me, as we share such devastating losses that no mother ever expects to journey through. Judith, thank you for sharing your story that brought two mothers together. Thank you for reading and endorsing *Dear Heroin*. I am truly blessed.

I am indebted to Dr. Trudy M. Johnson, Certified Clinical Trauma Professional (CCTP-l), LMFT (a licensed marriage and family therapist) in the State of Colorado and Tennessee. She is the founder of A'nesis Retreats and Counseling Sabbaticals and she worked in a nationally known ministry from 1994 to 2005 reaching out to women with grief and abuse issues. I was a client of Trudy's, at Cross-Roads Counseling of the Rockies, for a two-week intensive session. She helped me work through several personal issues and gave wise counsel on Mike's addiction. We have kept in contact over the last few years. When I contacted her about endorsing my book, she graciously said yes. Trudy, your counseling skills and resources have kept me going throughout this roller coaster journey with Mikey. Thank you for your encouragement and making me feel I was not alone. Your kind and generous words endorsing my book mean so much to me. You are truly a light in the darkness.

Sometimes it's the behind-the-scenes things that happen before publication. I want to thank Jordyn at Wow Bar, Minneapolis, for her expertise in applying makeup and styling hair prior to having my author picture taken. It was a relaxing time and I felt very pampered. Kudos, Jordyn.

I want to thank my good friend, Sandi Holmgren of Holmgren Design, for her skill and expertise in photography. We spent an afternoon together catching up while she took over 150 pictures. We have been friends for over twenty years. We met through church. When I became an LPN, I took care of her son, Anders, who was born with pseudo-obstruction of the bowels, until his untimely death at age two. Another momma who has experienced the unthinkable. Sandi, thank you for taking my picture and the friendship we share.

I want to thank Women of Words (WOW 1) for their support, encouragement, and mentoring me through this writing journey. This community of women are committed to help and support one another, personally and professionally as writers. It is a privilege to be a part of this group of dynamic women who have positively impacted me. Thank you all so very much.

A big thank you to all those who sent me "Mikey" stories via email, snail mail, or by conversations over the phone. I learned so much about Mike and his life in Colorado, his drug use and even his last few conversations before leaving this world. Many I have used in the book, others I will add to my website. Your stories brought laughter, tears, and much joy. I am so very grateful for each and every one I have received. My heartfelt thanks to you all.

Without a doubt I am most thankful to God, my Savior. I have walked with the Lord since I was a young girl. My foundation is my faith in Christ. Without that, I don't know where I'd be in my life. I don't know how I would navigate my daily life without His love, His constant reassurance and the knowledge that He has never left me, abandoned me, or turned His back on me, even when I have been less than faithful to Him. My faith has grown since Mikey's death. I don't know how anyone can survive the death of a child without some kind of faith in God or a higher power. I know I could not do this on my own or in my own strength. All those Bible verses I learned about God's love and care have been tested over the last few years. But I can say without a doubt, without fear, that God's word is truth and He is faithful. I thank Him every day for the life I have been given and everything that comes with it. All the joy, all the good, all the sad, all the difficult, and even with Mike's death I am grateful. When I pray, I cup my hands in front of me as a reminder to hold loosely the things in this life because I never know what may come next. Thank you, Lord, for all that you have given me. May I be forever grateful.

To my family:

I want to thank my mom, Betty, for helping me understand some of the encounters she had with Mike during his journey, some of which I lacked knowledge of. Most importantly I want to thank her for her support, encouragement, and unconditional love. Mom, you have walked beside me in this journey. I have relied on you so very often. I love the times we've spent sitting at your dining room table sharing our lives, from the mundane events to the incredibly important ones. You have been a role model for me as I watched you take care of Dad for so many years, especially his last few months on earth. You have guided me as a mother, especially when you saw me making errors raising my children. You always offered counsel in your loving manner. I didn't understand the impact that losing a grandchild could have. Now that I have my own, I can't imagine losing him under any circumstances. The void would be unimaginable.

Thank you, Mom. I love you very much.

To my sisters, Candee and Tracy. I want to thank you for allowing me to add your stories about Mike and your relationship with him in the written word. As the eldest, by many years, it has been a joy and pleasure to watch you grow into the beautiful, loving, Godly women you are. I have watched you get married, have and raise my nieces and nephews. All of whom have grown or are growing into strong, responsible, loving, and caring individuals. We have had so many crazy adventures together. We have laughed until we nearly peed ourselves. We have held each other and cried buckets of tears. It is the challenges in our lives that have kept us so very close in spirit and in heart, though we are miles apart. I have prayed for you both as long as I can remember. I know you pray for me in return. Thank you so very much for being two of the best Sistos ever. Here's to many more times and adventures in the years to come.

I love you both to the moon and back.

To Sean: I love the relationship we have. It has become closer over the last several years. I love the way we talk smack to each other on a daily basis. I love giving you crap about being my "favorite" middle child. Yet you are the one I talk most seriously with. You listen to me as I ramble on about my day, my ups and downs. You understand my heart and I am very grateful for that. You have answered my questions about your relationship with Mike and have pulled up some painful memories, which you've shared with me. I remember our first Christmas after Mike died. We stood in front of the Christmas tree and held on to each other and wept. As we have journeyed forward, I have seen healing in your soul. It has been my joy to interact with you as an adult, not a child. You have an amazing sense of humor, and you are so gifted in many areas. I find myself looking at you some days, blown away by your intelligence, good looks, your understanding of computers and technology. You are my "go to" guy when I need help with my phone or the computer. But it's your kind and generous heart that makes me love you so very much. I look forward to the years ahead as you continue your journey into adulthood.

Thank you for being such a remarkable son. I love you so very much.

To Dan: You are my first born, our experiment as we learned to parent on you. (Hopefully we haven't screwed you up too badly.) You are a typical first-born. You will confront and take charge of any given situation. You are black and white, with little grey in your thoughts and judgments. And you do not sugar coat your words, and I love that about you, so completely opposite of me. You have been my rock and strength as we have journeyed through Mike's life, addiction, and suicide. In the aftermath of it, you have healed as much as one can. It has been my pleasure to watch you grow and mature into the amazing man you are. In the last three years I have had the pleasure of watching you become a husband and father. I have seen you grow into your role of a loving and caring husband. And you are such a nurturing father to that little boy, and I love watching you and Lindsey parent him as you work together building a good life for yourselves. I do get a sick satisfaction watching how Karma comes back to bite you in the butt as you wrestle with a strong-willed first born. I don't think I would have gotten through those first painful days, weeks and months without you and your love holding me up.

Thank you for being my rock. I love you very very much.

To Allan: My husband, partner, lover, friend, dad, and papa. I have been blessed to have the privilege of walking beside you for nearly forty-six years. You are an incredible husband. You are physically and emotionally strong. You are forthright, you examine every situation from as many perspectives as possible before making a final decision. You take your time, and you don't hurry the outcome of any given situation. You always plan ahead, and you prepare for all kinds of situations. That is your strength. At the same time, you are tender and caring. I see that in how you nurture Little Man and those around you. You are willing to help others, even if it means stopping or giving up something you are doing. And you love our family, you love me. I can see that love in your eyes. I see that love in how you do those little things for me that make my life easier. You bring me flowers, give cute cards, and bring me my favorite Blizzards from DQ. You watched over me while I went through many unpleasant situations early in our marriage. You have shown me how to love with your kind gestures. You make me laugh every single day.

You were strong when we found out about Mike and his addiction and you did everything you could to help him. You stood beside him and loved him unconditionally those last four years of his life even though it was so very painful to watch Mike cycle up and down and eventually end his life.

You have supported my endeavor to write this book. You answered my questions when I couldn't remember. You had to drag up those painful memories in order for me to piece together parts that were missing. You had to "dig deep." One of the biggest and hardest things you did was spend a day reading my manuscript. You read it cover to cover and made notes and added parts that were incomplete or missing. You were drained by the end of that long day. Yet you never complained about doing it. I am so grateful for that. This book is much richer for having you do that. You added so much to the story that would have been otherwise missed.

Our marriage and life are stronger because of the faith you possess in God. Your faith has never wavered.

Thank you for all the love and support you have given me throughout our life together but especially the past thirteen years.

I love you forever and always. I can't imagine my life without you. I look forward to the years ahead, Lord willing we will have many.

Service Material from the General Service Office

The Twelve Steps of Alcoholics Anonymous

1. We admitted we were powerless over alcohol—that our lives had become unmanageable.

2. Came to believe that a Power greater than ourselves could restore us to sanity.

3. Made a decision to turn our will and our lives over to the care of God *as we understood Him.*

4. Made a searching and fearless moral inventory of ourselves.

5. Admitted to God, to ourselves, and to another human being the exact nature of our wrongs.

6. Were entirely ready to have God remove all these defects of character.

7. Humbly asked Him to remove our shortcomings.

8. Made a list of all persons we had harmed, and became willing to make amends to them all.

9. Made direct amends to such people wherever possible, except when to do so would injure them or others.

10. Continued to take personal inventory and when we were wrong promptly admitted it.

11. Sought through prayer and meditation to improve our conscious contact with God *as we understood Him*, praying only for knowledge of His will for us and the power to carry that out.

12. Having had a spiritual awakening as the result of these steps, we tried to carry this message to alcoholics and to practice these principles in all our affairs.

The Serenity Prayer

God grant me the serenity
to accept the things I cannot change,
courage to change the things I can,
and wisdom to know the difference.
Living one day at a time;
enjoying one moment at a time;
accepting hardships as the pathway to peace;
taking, as He did, this sinful world
as it is, not as I would have it;
trusting that He will make all things right
if I surrender to His Will;
that I may be reasonably happy in this life
and supremely happy with Him
forever in the next.
Amen.

—Reinhold Niebuhr (1892–1971)

Notes

1. National Institute on Drug Abuse (NIDA), "What is the Scope of Heroin Use in the United States?" May 29, 2020, https://www.drugabuse.gov/publications/research-reports/heroin/scope-heroin-use-in-united-states.

2. Jeffrey Juergens, "Suicide and Substance Abuse," Addiction Center, last modified November 20, 2020, https://www.addictioncenter.com/addiction/addiction-and-suicide.

3. Carolyn C. Ross, "Suicide: One of Addiction's Hidden Risks," *Psychology Today*, February 20, 2014, https://www.psychologytoday.com/us/blog/real-healing/201402/suicide-one-addiction-s-hidden-risks.

4. North Country Canoe Outfitters, "About the Boundary Waters Canoe Area Wilderness (BWCA)," https://boundarywaters.com/boundary-waters/.

5. "Heroin Withdrawal Effects," Heroin.net, last modified May 28, 2020, https://heroin.net/information-heroin-addiction/withdrawal/heroin-withdrawal-effects.

6. "What is A.A.?" Alcoholics Anonymous, https://www.aa.org/pages/en_US/what-is-aa.

7. Melissa Conrad Stöppler, "Is Your Child or Teen Huffing?" MedicineNet, https://www.medicinenet.com/is_your_child_or_teen_huffing/views.htm.

8. Jeffrey Juergens, "Inpatient vs. Outpatient," Addiction Center, last modified September 18, 2020, https://www.addictioncenter.com/treatment/inpatient-outpatient-rehab/.

9. Beverly Conyers, "Are You Addicted to Your Addicted Child?" MomPower, https://mompower.org/wp-content/uploads/2019/11/Are-You-Addicted-to-Your-Addicted-ChildQuiz_BeverlyConyers.pdf.

10. "Cues Give Clues in Relapse Prevention," National Institute on Drug Abuse, April 8, 2019, https://www.drugabuse.gov/news-events/science-highlight/cues-give-clues-in-relapse-prevention.

11. Steven M. Melemis, "Relapse Prevention Plan and Early Warning Signs," Addictions and Recovery, last modified October 31, 2020, https://www.addictionsandrecovery.org/relapse-prevention.htm.

12. "What Is Cross-Addiction?" Hazelden Betty Ford Foundation, January 17, 2019, https://www.hazeldenbettyford.org/articles/what-is-cross-addiction.

13. Stephanie Mansour, "What Is CrossFit? And Is It Right for You? Here's What You Need to Know," November 8, 2019, https://www.nbcnews.com/better/lifestyle/what-crossfit-it-right-you-here-s-what-you-need-ncna1070886.

14. Eckhart Tolle, *The Power of Now: A Guide to Spiritual Enlightenmen*t, rev. ed. (Novato, Calif.: New World Library, 2004), 13.

15. Destiny Bezrutczyk, "Speedball" Addiction Center, last modified November 20, 2020, https://www.addictioncenter.com/drugs/heroin/speedball.

About the Author

Linda Morrison was born and raised in Colorado Springs, Colorado. She lived there until her marriage to Allan Morrison, an Air Force Academy graduate, in 1975. They moved around the country until Allan left the air force in 1982. They moved to Saint Paul, Minnesota, where they raised their three sons. Linda was a stay-at-home mom until she went to nursing school in 1998. After becoming a licensed practical nurse, she worked in hospitals and clinics and did homecare until she retired in 2016. She loves reading novels, memoirs, and nonfiction, and she is an avid biker and walker; she has completed two half-marathons. Her greatest joy is spending time with her young grandson.

Mike's addiction and death in 2012 changed her world. A speaker and author, she is now an advocate for those caught in the circle of substance abuse, and she encourages and supports families walking this journey. This is her first book.

Light One Candle LLC
Dear Heroin - A Memoir
Linda Morrison